Puzzle Packing Companies
Expanding Place Value

Diana Gomez

Sharon Askew

Andrea L'Tainen

Catherine Twomey Fosnot

New Perspectives on Learning, LLC
1194 Ocean Avenue
New London, CT 06320

ISBN-13: 978-1-7320437-3-2

Table of Contents

Unit Overview

The focus of this unit is the extension of children's understanding of place value. CFLM units in the place value strand for earlier grades (*Organizing and Collecting* and *The T-shirt Factory*) provided children with multiple opportunities to explore additive structuring: decomposition of amounts, expanded notation, regrouping and equivalence. This unit is designed as a bridge from additive structuring to multiplicative structuring of the number system, and extends place value to 1,000,000. It also fosters a deep understanding of the standard algorithms for addition and subtraction. The unit is designed to align with the CCSS Standards of Practice and the following core objectives:

Numbers & Operations in Base Ten 4.NBT[1]

Generalize place value understanding for multi-digit whole numbers.

CCSS.MATH.CONTENT.4.NBT.A.1

Recognize that in a multi-digit whole number, a digit in one place represents ten times what it represents in the place to its right.

CCSS.MATH.CONTENT.4.NBT.A.2

Read and write multi-digit whole numbers using base-ten numerals, number names, and expanded form. Compare two multi-digit numbers based on meanings of the digits in each place, using >, =, and < symbols to record the results of comparisons.

CCSS.MATH.CONTENT.4.NBT.A.3

Use place value understanding to round multi-digit whole numbers to any place.

Use place value understanding and properties of operations to perform multi-digit arithmetic.

CCSS.MATH.CONTENT.4.NBT.B.4

Fluently add and subtract multi-digit whole numbers using the standard algorithms.

The Mathematical Landscape

Puzzle Packing Companies is designed to support the further development of place value by involving students in structuring the number system with powers of ten and extending their work with numbers to 1,000,000. In previous grades, students most likely developed an understanding of the decomposition and equivalence of amounts and expanded notation. Hopefully, your students can now think of 132, for example, as 1 hundred + 3 tens + 2 units, or as 13 tens + 2 units, or as 12 tens + 12 units, etc. and they

---

[1] Grade 4 expectations in this domain are limited to whole numbers less than or equal to 1,000,000.

know these are all equivalent amounts. This unit extends that understanding to foster the envisioning of our number system multiplicatively. Our place value system is a beautiful invention. It is a system based on the powers of ten, where a digit in one place represents ten times what it represents in the place to its right. Understanding place value deeply is required to understand why the standard algorithms for addition and subtraction work.

Liping Ma (1999) compared the way Chinese teachers think about and teach place value and the computation algorithms for addition and subtraction based on place value, to the way American teachers usually proceed with these topics. Chinese teachers tend to focus far more on the maintaining of equivalence throughout the regrouping, whereas U.S. teachers tend to proceed step-by-step, starting with the units, and teaching regrouping as a procedure. U.S. teachers also tend to focus on helping children line up numbers in columns and to treat these columns one at a time. In contrast, Chinese teachers first develop a deep understanding of expanded notation and equivalence. For example, they focus on how 141=100+40+1=100+30+11. In later years, they focus on the multiplicative understandings of the base system, where 141 is understood to be equivalent to 14.1 tens, and to 1.41 hundreds. The addition and subtraction algorithms then fall out naturally as students use partial sums and partial differences of powers of ten to calculate total sums and differences.

This unit is designed to help students explore the structure and regularity, and ultimately the elegance, of our place value system. As such, it is an important bridge to understanding decimals, which will be a focus in grade 5. Although an understanding of the regrouping algorithms for addition and subtraction is one of the goals of this unit, they are primarily being developed to deepen students' understanding of our place value system and to explore the beauty of the generalizable strategies for addition and subtraction that emerge because of the structuring of the number system with powers of ten.

Written algorithms—such as the borrowing and carrying procedures for adding and subtracting—were made popular by the great Arab mathematician Muhammad ibn Musa al-Khwarizmi in the early part of the ninth century. (His Latin name was Algorismus—hence the term algorithm.) With the development of regrouping based on place value (borrowing and carrying procedures), computations could be carried out directly with a pen and papyrus. The power of the procedures was that they produced a record of the actions and results could now be checked; calculating was no longer restricted to the guild of professional calculators using the abacus.

Arithmetic procedures and the computational writing that documented them became the hallmark of knowledge during the Renaissance because these skills were now required in the marketplace. Hence, they became the focus of instruction for students through the elementary years. The algorithms have continued to be the goal of arithmetic instruction in our schools ever since, primarily because, until the proliferation of calculators, they were the fastest, most efficient way to compute long columns and thus they were viewed as a characteristic of numeracy. Today however, we can just ask Siri or Cortana (they are on our cellphone or watch), or we can use the handheld calculator (which is also rapidly becoming outdated) to do computations. However, we do have to be able to assess whether the answer on the calculator is reasonable. We do have to have good mental arithmetic strategies based on place value and the properties of operations to judge the reasonableness of answers—the new definition of numeracy. A deep understanding of number and operation, place value, powers and exponents, and base systems are an important foundation for algebra, also, and for that reason alone, developing a strong understanding of place value needs to be taken seriously.

This unit is specifically crafted to add the standard algorithms for addition and subtraction to the repertoire of strategies for computation developed by this series. These algorithms, however, are not seen as the ultimate strategies for computation, only as other (albeit generalizable) strategies based on a deep sense of number and operation. The important underlying ideas to emphasize as you work through this unit are place value, powers of ten, and equivalence—not computational procedures. Clever alternative mental arithmetic strategies should not be abandoned in place of the pencil/paper algorithms being developed here. Numerate people always look to the numbers first and vary their strategies accordingly. Allow your students to do the same, but make use of the context to develop an understanding of the standard algorithms that emerge. As you work through this unit there are several big ideas, strategies, and models on the landscape to encourage and celebrate.

The Landscape of Learning

BIG IDEAS
❖ Unitizing
❖ Place determines value
❖ Equivalence with place value
❖ Place value patterns occur when multiplying by ten
❖ Commutative Property
❖ Associative Property
❖ Place value positions are related by powers of ten
❖ Multiplication and division by ten make the whole shift to the left and to the right
❖ With powers of ten, the exponent tells how many times 10 has been multiplied by itself, and therefore also how many zeros there will be in the product
❖ When multiplying powers of ten, one can add the exponents
❖ When dividing powers of ten, one can subtract the exponents
❖ The shapes of powers of ten repeat in periods

STRATEGIES
❖ Splitting
❖ Rounding multi-digit whole numbers and adjusting
❖ Regrouping, but inefficiently
❖ Using the standard addition algorithm flexibly and efficiently
❖ Using the standard subtraction algorithm flexibly and efficiently
❖ Skip counting
❖ Using ten-times

- ❖ Using multiples of powers of ten as partial products or quotients
- ❖ Simplifying
- ❖ Using place value and properties of operations to multiply and divide by powers of ten

MODELS

- ❖ Additive structuring
- ❖ Multiplicative structuring
- ❖ Base-ten blocks

BIG IDEAS

As children explore the investigations within this unit, several big ideas will likely arise. These include:

- ❖ *Unitizing*
- ❖ *Place determines value*
- ❖ *Equivalence with place value*
- ❖ *Place value patterns occur when multiplying by ten*
- ❖ *Commutative Property*
- ❖ *Associative Property*
- ❖ *Place value positions are related by powers of ten*
- ❖ *Multiplication and division by ten make the whole shift to the left and to the right*
- ❖ *With powers of ten, the exponent tells how many times 10 has been multiplied by itself, and therefore also how many zeros there will be in the product*
- ❖ *When multiplying powers of ten, one can add the exponents*
- ❖ *When dividing powers of ten, one can subtract the exponents*
- ❖ *The shapes of powers of ten repeat in periods*

❖ Unitizing

Unitizing requires that children use number to count not only objects but also groups—and to count them both simultaneously. For young learners, unitizing is a shift in perspective. Children have just learned to count ten objects, one by one. Unitizing these ten objects as one thing—one group—requires almost negating their original idea of number. How can something be ten and one at the same time? As children explore ways to make groups, and then groups of groups, they develop ways to unitize the group—they treat a group of ten as a unit, and ten groups of ten (100 units) as one unit of a hundred.

❖ Place determines value

The idea that a numeral can represent ones or tens or hundreds depending on where it is placed is what we mean by place value. The numeral "2" may represent two units, but the units themselves can change; they can be ones or tens or hundreds or more. The unit varies—its amount changes depending on the column in which the digit is placed.

❖ Equivalence with place value

By the time they start working with this unit, children may have constructed the idea that amounts can be rearranged and decomposed and still be equivalent. They often need to revisit this idea, however, when they begin to explore place value with greater amounts. Understanding the equivalence of 2 pallets, 3 long boxes, and 2 loose puzzle cubes to 23 long boxes and 2 loose cubes, or to 22 long boxes and 12 loose cubes may at first be somewhat elusive.

❖ Place value patterns occur when multiplying by ten

An interesting thing happens when we multiply by the base—the factor bumps over to the appropriate column. For example, 10x4 = 4+4+4+4+4+4+4+4+4+4. The result of 40 seems like magic to students, who often say that they added a zero to the 4. When challenged, they will agree they did not really "add" a zero; they just placed it on the right of the number they were multiplying. Noticing this pattern is important, but sadly most students have little understanding of why this pattern occurs. The reason this action works is that we can think of the ten groups of four as four groups of ten (the commutative property)—so the 4 is placed (bumps over) into the tens column. Likewise, 100x8 = 8x100, so the 8 bumps over to the hundreds place. It is important to support students in exploring why this pattern happens—to help them construct how place value and the commutative property are involved.

❖ Commutative property

Multiplication is commutative: a x b = b x a. Picture four towers, each made with nineteen connecting cubes. Now imagine them right next to each other so they make a 4x19 rectangular array. If we turn this array ninety degrees, we have a 19x4 array—nineteen towers with four cubes in each. Using arrays like this is exactly what students do to convince each other of the commutative property. Students may have constructed this property earlier, but they may not have related it to the place value patterns that occur when multiplying by ten. For this reason, we have placed it here on the place value landscape.

❖ Associative property

As your students work with the investigations in this unit, they will begin to understand that 10x10 results in 100 and 10x10x10 results in 1000. They will also begin to realize that, because of the commutative property, 1,000x100 can also be 100x1,000, which results in 100,000. Another way to explore this with your students as you confer is to make use of the associative property: (10x10x10)x(10x10) = (10x10)x(10x10x10). Only the parentheses have moved. In fact, the parentheses can be moved to a variety of places because the associative property holds for multiplication: 10x(10x10x10x10) = 100,000.

❖ Place value positions are related by powers of ten

As students construct an understanding of place value, they learn that a number like 249 contains 24 tens, with 9 more ones. It is also equivalent to 24.9 tens if we think of the 9 as a fractional part of 10, or 2490 tenths. Students usually aren't introduced to decimals until grade 5, but this unit lays the foundation for an understanding of decimals by developing a deep understanding of how place value positions are related by powers of ten. Each new puzzle cube box is 10 tens bigger than the one prior.

❖ *Multiplication and division by ten make the whole shift to the left and to the right*

The beauty of our base-ten system is that when multiplying or dividing by 10, we only need to shift to the right or to the left, depending on the operation: 249/10 = 24.9; 249x10 = 2490. One truckload of 1,000,000 cubes can simultaneously be seen as 1,000 shipping boxes of 1,000 cubes (1,000x1,000), 10 giant pallets of 100,000 cubes (10x100,000), or as 100,000 long boxes of tens (100,000x10).

❖ *With powers of ten, the exponent tells how many times 10 has been multiplied by itself, and therefore also how many zeros there will be in the product*

Students are naturally introduced to exponents in this unit when they begin to realize that a number like 1,000 is also 10x10x10. This is not the same thing as 3x10; it is 10 multiplied by itself 3 times, written as 10^3. Students will be amazed when they discover that 1 million is 10^6, and that there are 6 zeros because every time a number is scaled up by 10, a zero is placed to bump the number over to the next place on the left.

❖ *When multiplying powers of ten, one can add the exponents*

Precisely because with powers of ten the exponents express how many times 10 has been multiplied by itself, a power of ten times another power of ten can be determined by just adding the exponents: for example, $10^2 \times 10^6 = 10^8$

❖ *When dividing powers of ten, one can subtract the exponents*

Because division is the inverse of multiplication, when dividing a power of ten by another power of ten, one can subtract the exponents: for example, $10^6 / 10^2 = 10^4$.

❖ *The shapes of powers of ten repeat in periods*

In our base-ten system, numbers are expressed in periods. The periods are most often expressed by commas (at least in the U.S.) and after every third column we place a comma. For example, let's examine one million: 1,000,000. The clustering or grouping of three columns between the commas is purposeful. It shows the periodicity of units, thousands, millions, billions, etc. In this unit, students explore box designs that are scaled up each time by ten. Since the first unit box is a small cube, the first box in the next period will also be a cube, but that cube is 1,000 times larger than the unit. The shapes within the periods progress from cube (1), to long (10), to pallet (100). The next period is 1,000 times larger but the shape repeats: cube, long, pallet. One million must of course then be a giant cube, 1,000 times larger than 1,000 and 1,000,000 times larger than the unit cube.

As you work with the activities in this unit, you will notice that students will use many strategies to solve the problems that are posed to them. Here are some strategies to notice:

- ❖ *Splitting*
- ❖ *Rounding multi-digit whole numbers and adjusting*
- ❖ *Regrouping, but inefficiently*
- ❖ *Using the standard addition algorithm flexibly and efficiently*
- ❖ *Using the standard subtraction algorithm flexibly and efficiently*
- ❖ *Skip counting*
- ❖ *Using ten-times*
- ❖ *Using multiples of powers of ten as partial products or quotients*
- ❖ *Simplifying*
- ❖ *Using place value and properties of operations to multiply and divide by powers of ten*

❖ *Splitting*

When children decompose numbers using expanded notation, they split numbers up into partial sums to add and into partial differences to subtract. We call this strategy "splitting," meaning that the numbers are split by place value position and expressed in expanded notation. For example, 133 + 29 might be solved as: 30 + 20 + 3 + 9 + 100, and 133-29 might be solved as 30 - 20 + 3 - 9 + 100. In earlier grades, the development of these strategies was cause for celebration as they show an understanding of expanded notation. However, these strategies are cumbersome, requiring many parts to remember and some focused thinking on whether to add or subtract pieces (particularly when doing partial differences). As their understanding of place value deepens, children will likely begin to abandon splitting and opt for more efficient strategies that require a smaller memory load when calculating.

❖ *Rounding multi-digit whole numbers and adjusting*

When adding or subtracting, it is usually more efficient to keep one number whole and round an addend or subtrahend to a nearby landmark number and then adjust, than it is to use splitting. For example, 133+29 might now be solved as 133+30-1; and 133-29 might be solved as 133-30+1. Keeping one number whole and rounding others to a landmark number is also based on place value as this understanding helps children know which place to round to. This strategy also helps with judging the reasonableness of an answer and with estimating.

❖ *Regrouping, but inefficiently*

Regrouping is the basis for the standard algorithms for addition and subtraction. Rather than keeping numbers whole and rounding and adjusting, the algorithms make use of a decomposition based on a deep understanding of the multiplicative nature of our base-ten system. For that reason, the CCSS does not require the use of the algorithms based on regrouping until grade 4 because they are the most difficult for children to understand. Regrouping requires the use of partial sums and differences, but the pieces also need to be understood multiplicatively (as multiplied by powers of ten) to know what the digits in the columns stand for. Several big ideas underlie the standard regrouping algorithms for addition and subtraction. Using these strategies with meaning demands that children unitize groups, know that place determines value, and understand equivalence and associativity (3 tens + 4 ones is equivalent to 2 tens + 14 ones). When regrouping methods are taught as rote procedures, children often latch on to them without understanding deeply why they work. Make sure as you work with this unit that you emphasize equivalence, and support students in observing that partial sums (the sums of addends of the same place value) can be added and regrouped to determine the total sum. As students begin to explore regrouping within contexts that require it (like the ones about boxes in this unit), they often begin inefficiently and regroup several times. For example, when adding they may start on the left and add and then regroup several times before they arrive at a correct answer. When subtracting, they may regroup in every column, even when not necessary, and then regroup again to get to their answer. See the samples provided in Figure 1.

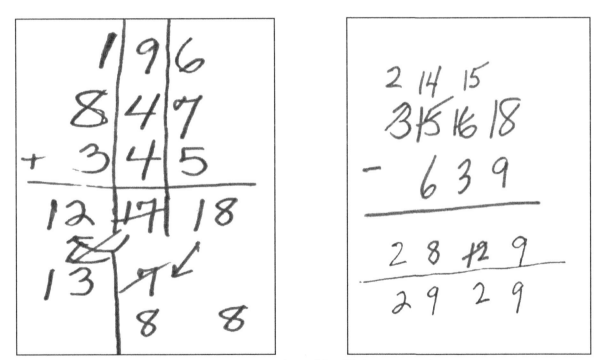

Figure 1. Two samples of inefficient grouping.

❖ Using the standard addition algorithm flexibly and efficiently

As students continue exploring regrouping with addition, they develop a very strong sense of equivalence and their strategies become more efficient. They learn that regrouping isn't necessary all the time and they look more carefully at the numbers. They come to realize that if they start on the right and regroup only when needed, then when they finish on the left the work is already organized and regrouped minimally.

❖ Using the standard subtraction algorithm flexibly and efficiently

As students continue exploring regrouping with subtraction, some may continue to work left to right and regroup very efficiently at the bottom, rather than at the top. For example, Figure 2 shows the work of a student who worked from the left first where no regrouping was required. Initially he had written "3" in the tens column, but upon realizing the units would require a ten to be regrouped, he removed the needed group of tens from the 3, leaving 2 tens, and mentally placed it in the units column (at first with the 8, but he quickly scratched this out). Other students learn that it is more efficient to move right to left, regrouping only as necessary. Still others regroup mentally as needed (see Figure 3), or even regroup multiple columns at once (see Figure 4).

Unpacking/Repacking Area	Shipping cubes	Pallets	Long Boxes	Loose Units
Beginning Totals →	5	5	7	0
Transaction:		4	4	2
What's left on the truck	5	1	8 2	8

Figure 2. Regrouping flexibly from the bottom when needed.

Unpacking/Repacking Area	Shipping cubes	Pallets	Long Boxes	Loose Units	
Beginning Totals →	8	1	a	3	8 9 8 / 7 6 9
Transaction: Gabe's Garage		5	7	4	

Figure 3. Regrouping mentally as needed.

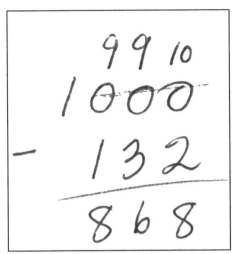

Figure 4. Regrouping 100 tens all at once into 99 tens, placing the ten remaining in the units column.

❖ Skip counting

To figure out the length of one hundred 3"x3"x3" puzzle cubes, you may find some students still skip counting—a counting strategy they developed much earlier. If so, encourage them to make use of place value and use 100x3, or at least 10x3 ten times.

❖ Using ten-times

Once students begin to make use of partial products, an important strategy to encourage is the use of the ten-times partial product. Of course, this strategy is helpful only if students have constructed an understanding of the place value patterns that occur when multiplying by the base; otherwise it is not an easy partial product to calculate.

❖ Using multiples of powers of ten as partial products or quotients

As children become more familiar with place value and the associative property, they will begin to solve problems using the properties in the following ways: 30 x 40, as 3x10x4x10 = 3x4x100; and 840/70 as 700/70 + 140/70.

❖ Simplifying

When dividing, one of the most powerful strategies to use when the dividend and divisor have common factors is simplification, or scaling: 700/70 = 70/7; likewise 300/12 = 100/4 and 170/5 = 340/10 = 34/1. Substituting and exchanging one expression for an equivalent one can often make the computation easy to do mentally.

❖ Using place value to multiply and divide by powers of ten

As students construct a deeper understanding of place value and are introduced to exponents, many new possibilities for computation open up. They begin to be able to make use of just shifting to the left or the right to multiply and divide by 10. For example, 3214/100 = 32.14 (one just needs to shift the number to the right 2 columns, thereby inserting the decimal point); and 3214 x 100 = 321,400 (one now just shifts the number 2 places to the left, inserting 2 zeros.) Exponents add even more computational power: $32{,}000 \times 1{,}500{,}000 = 32 \times 10^3 \times 15 \times 10^5 = 32 \times 15 \times 10^8 = 16 \times 30 \times 10^8 = 16 \times 3 \times 10^9 = 48{,}000{,}000{,}000$. Place value and powers of ten add such power! One doesn't even need to ask Siri or Cortana for an answer!

MATHEMATICAL MODELING

❖ Additive structuring

The first modeling of the number system on the landscape is additive. Children are challenged just by decomposing amounts. They do not see 132 as 13 tens + 2. They see it as 100 + 30 + 2. They decompose using expanded notation. When adding 132 + 146 they will likely model the problem additively, using splitting: 100 + 100 + 30 + 40 + 2 + 6.

❖ Multiplicative structuring

As students begin to understand that each column in our number system has been scaled by ten, and that shifting to the left or to the right is an efficient way to multiply or divide by ten, they no longer are structuring the system additively. They are now structuring it multiplicatively: 132 is seen as 13.2 tens, or as 1.32 hundreds. It is also 132×10^0, or 13.2×10^1, or 1.32×10^2.

❖ Base-Ten Blocks

In this unit base-ten blocks are used initially as a manipulative to allow students to model the box situation and to explore how the boxes are related to each other. However, the context is designed to promote a more schematic model of the blocks as a tool for thinking in the same way that in previous CFLM units, number lines and arrays became schematic models and tools for thinking using open number lines and open arrays. As you work with the activities in this unit, you will likely see children drawing boxes (not in scale) and using these as tools. This is purposeful in the design of the unit. The more schematic use of base-ten blocks (in contrast to the actual manipulatives) that evolves from the context invites students to imagine how the shapes (cube, long, and pallet) repeat in each period, how exponents determine the number of zeros, and how each period is 1,000 times larger than the one to its right, or 1,000 times smaller than the one to its left. In contrast to using the base-ten blocks as a manipulative to get an answer, the blocks are used initially as a representation *of* a situation; later they are used by teachers in quick images and to represent children's strategies. Ultimately, they are appropriated by children as powerful tools *for* thinking (Gravemeijer 1999). Scaled drawings do not matter; the drawings are purely schematic and used as a tool for thinking.

References and Resources

Gravemeijer, Koeno (1999). How emergent models may foster the constitution of formal mathematics. *Mathematical Thinking and Learning 1* (2): 155–77.

Ma, Liping (1999). Knowing and Teaching Elementary Mathematics: Teachers' Understanding of Fundamental Mathematics in China and the United States. Mahwah, New Jersey: Lawrence Erlbaum.

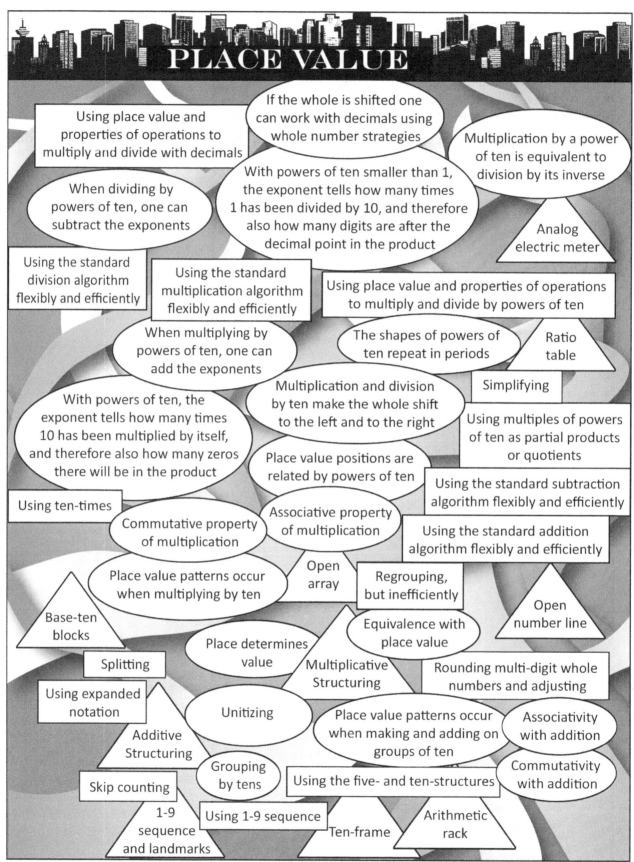

PLACE VALUE

Using place value and properties of operations to multiply and divide with decimals

If the whole is shifted one can work with decimals using whole number strategies

Multiplication by a power of ten is equivalent to division by its inverse

When dividing by powers of ten, one can subtract the exponents

With powers of ten smaller than 1, the exponent tells how many times 1 has been divided by 10, and therefore also how many digits are after the decimal point in the product

Analog electric meter

Using the standard division algorithm flexibly and efficiently

Using the standard multiplication algorithm flexibly and efficiently

Using place value and properties of operations to multiply and divide by powers of ten

When multiplying by powers of ten, one can add the exponents

The shapes of powers of ten repeat in periods

Ratio table

Simplifying

With powers of ten, the exponent tells how many times 10 has been multiplied by itself, and therefore also how many zeros there will be in the product

Multiplication and division by ten make the whole shift to the left and to the right

Using multiples of powers of ten as partial products or quotients

Place value positions are related by powers of ten

Using the standard subtraction algorithm flexibly and efficiently

Using ten-times

Commutative property of multiplication

Associative property of multiplication

Using the standard addition algorithm flexibly and efficiently

Place value patterns occur when multiplying by ten

Open array

Regrouping, but inefficiently

Open number line

Base-ten blocks

Equivalence with place value

Splitting

Place determines value

Multiplicative Structuring

Rounding multi-digit whole numbers and adjusting

Using expanded notation

Unitizing

Place value patterns occur when making and adding on groups of ten

Associativity with addition

Additive Structuring

Grouping by tens

Using the five- and ten-structures

Commutativity with addition

Skip counting

1-9 sequence and landmarks

Using 1-9 sequence

Ten-frame

Arithmetic rack

The landscape of learning: place value on the horizon showing landmark strategies (rectangles), big ideas (ovals), and models (triangles).

DAY ONE

BOXING PUZZLE CUBES

Materials Needed

Sample cube puzzles

Possible Box Designs (Appendix A)

Base-10 blocks, one set per pair of students consisting of: *1 Block of 1,000*
10 Flats of 100
10 Rods of 10
10 unit cubes

Scissors (one per pair of students)

Glue sticks

Chart or poster paper

Math Journals

Markers and Pencils

The context of designing boxes for puzzle cubes sets the stage for the deepening and extension of an understanding of place value. Students are introduced to types of plastic cubes that a company might make and shown pictures of some possible box designs that a factory might use when shipping out orders. Students work in pairs investigating how many cubes each box will hold.

Day One Outline

Developing the Context

❖ Introduce the context of a company making and shipping cube puzzles.

❖ Show pictures of some possible boxes a warehouse might use to ship cubes (Appendix A).

❖ Ask students to work in pairs to figure out how many cubes each box holds.

Supporting the Investigation

❖ Provide base-ten blocks for students to model the problem as needed.

❖ As students work, move around and confer. Encourage them not to build each box and count, but to consider the multiplicative relationships between the boxes.

❖ Note the strategies students use to determine amounts.

Math Journals

❖ Provide a few minutes at the end of class for students to reflect and work to articulate their learning from the day and related inquiries they might wish to pursue.

Developing the Context

Later in this unit students will be engaged in a simulation game where they will take on the roles of employees at a company that manufactures, inventories, packs, and ships puzzle cubes. There are many types of puzzles in the shape of cubes on the market, for example there are 6-sided mazes with tiny balls inside and cubes with numerals on the faces that need to be arranged in order. Consider bringing in one or more of these puzzles (or use pictures from the internet) to help make the context more engaging for students. Ensure that any sample you bring in is a cube, however, as the shape is critical to the mathematics in the investigations.

Many teachers using this unit have found it helpful to use a Rubik's Cube®[2], as students at this age are often fascinated by the puzzle. If you decide to use a Rubik's Cube® you may want to search the web for some helpful background information to use as you develop the context. The internet is full of stories of the inventor, Ernő Rubik, and a quick search will provide you with many stories you can use. Show the cube or images of it and tell a bit about the inventor.

Professor Ernő Rubik, inventor of Rubik's Cube

Ernő Rubik was a professor and architect who taught design at the Academy of Applied Arts in Budapest, Hungary. One day, as he was searching for a way to demonstrate 3-D movement to his university students, he was staring into the River Danube looking at how the water moved around the pebbles, and he had an inspiration for the cube's twisting mechanism. The fact that the cube can twist without falling apart is part of its magic. He experimented in his mother's apartment, using wood, rubber bands, and paper clips to make a prototype. He needed some sort of coding to bring sense to the needed rotations of the cube, so he decided to use the simplest and strongest solution: primary colors. He has described his emotions as he first put stickers on the cube: "I felt very emotional. I knew it was revolutionary. The moment I started twisting the sides, I could see it was a proper puzzle—but what I didn't know was whether it could be solved. It took me weeks: there are 43 quintillion permutations!"

Explain that over the years many people have studied ways to solve the puzzle more quickly. Mathematics has helped them a lot and now several people have cracked ways to do the puzzle in only a few seconds! On the web, you can easily find several short video clips of the current record holders doing this. [Note: On P2S2: a personalized professional support system™ www.NewPerspectivesOnline.net, the online support system for CFLM, we provide an updated list of links for you.]

Once you have your students interested in puzzle cubes, explain that in a few days you will be involving them in a simulation game, where they will be pretending to be employees of a puzzle cube company. They will need to keep track of the company's inventory, the buying and selling, and the shipping. To get

---

[2] Rubik's Cube® used by permission Rubik's Brand Ltd. www.rubiks.com.

started it will be helpful to know something about how the cubes might be packaged and shipped. Display Appendix A, which shows the designs for boxes that the factories in the game will use when they ship cubes. Provide sets of base-ten blocks for each pair of students and send them off in pairs to determine how many cubes each box will hold.

Teacher Note:

Do not allow students to make designs of their own choosing. The math investigation is to determine how many cubes these specific boxes hold. There are several reasons the boxes are designed the way they are. For one, the box designs will foster new insights about place value and the resulting shape of the number as it scales by 10. Secondly, as students notice that each box is 10 times bigger than the previous one, they will also notice how the number of zeros (in the number of cubes) increases accordingly. This noticing leads to a big idea: every time a number is multiplied by 10 there is an equivalent way of thinking about it as that many tens ($10 \times n = n \times 10$), and therefore the digits in the number move over one place to the left and, with whole numbers, a zero is placed in the units column. This realization lays the foundation for understanding how and why exponents can be added to determine the number of zeros (and the exponent) in the product: $10^2 \times 10^2 = 10^4 = 10,000$. Finally, there is a specific reason that only a limited number of base-ten cubes are provided. There should be enough to get students started modeling the problem, but not enough to foster counting. With limited quantities, counting will become insufficient and students will need to begin to think multiplicatively to image the amounts and the shape of the boxes. At a minimum they will begin to skip count or use repeated addition, and soon these strategies will give way to multiplication as students see the place value patterns that result.

Supporting the Investigation

Let students get settled and ensure everyone understands the goal of the investigation. Then listen in on some conversations. Here are some strategies and big ideas you are likely to see emerging in the work:

❖ Noticing that, when you multiply a number by ten, the number moves to the left and a zero gets "added" in the units place. The big idea that explains why this happens is the commutative property: if one multiplies 10 x 100, this also equals 100 x 10, so the 100 moves over a place to show that there are now 100 tens. (See Figure 5.)

❖ Noticing that 10 x 10 x 10 x 10 x 10 can also be thought of as (10 x 10) x (10 x 10 x 10) or as 10 x (10 x 10 x 10 x 10), or as (10 x 10 x 10) x (10 x 10), etc. The big idea underlying this is the associative property. (See Figure 6.)

- ❖ Generalizing from the associative property to note that when multiplying powers of ten one only needs to place a number of zeros at the end equal to the sum of the powers of ten (the sum of the exponents). Note in Figure 7 how the students explain why $10^{11} \times 10^{11} = 10^{22}$.
- ❖ Noticing that the shape repeats (cube, long, pallet; big cube, big long, big pallet; giant cube, giant long, giant pallet; etc.). One, one thousand, one million, one billion, etc., are the powers of 10 that are multiples of 3 and can all be arranged in a cube shape. For example: $1,000 = 10^3$, $1,000,000 = 10^6$, because you are multiplying 1,000 by 1,000. See Figures 8a and 8b.

Figure 5. Noticing how the number of zeros increases and explaining it using the commutative property.

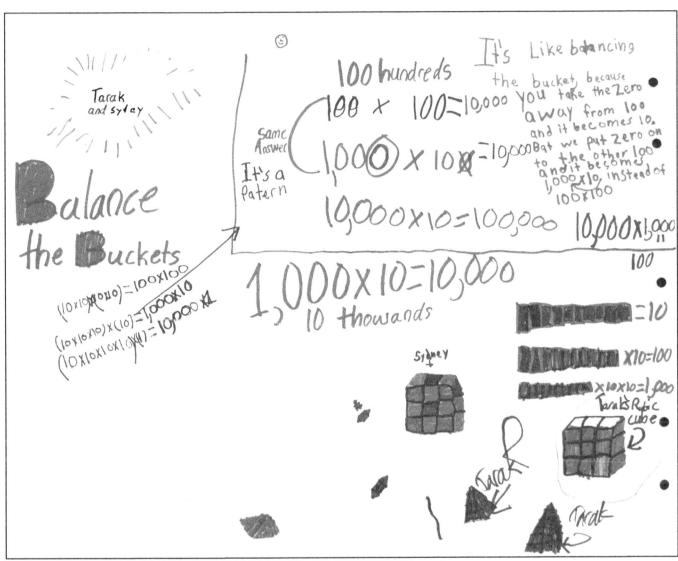

Figure 6. The Associative Property.

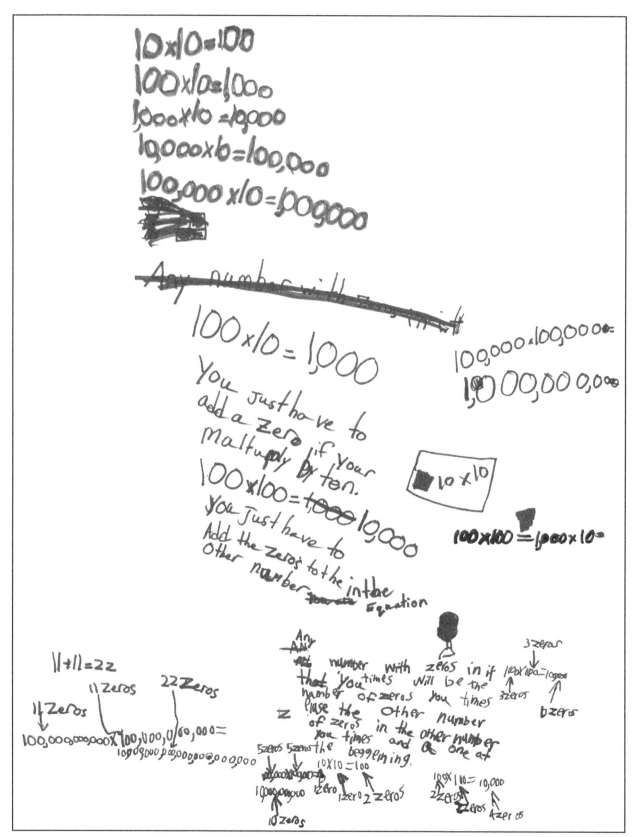

Figure 7. Extending from the associative property with the generalization that, when multiplying powers of 10, adding the exponents of the factors produces the exponent in the product.

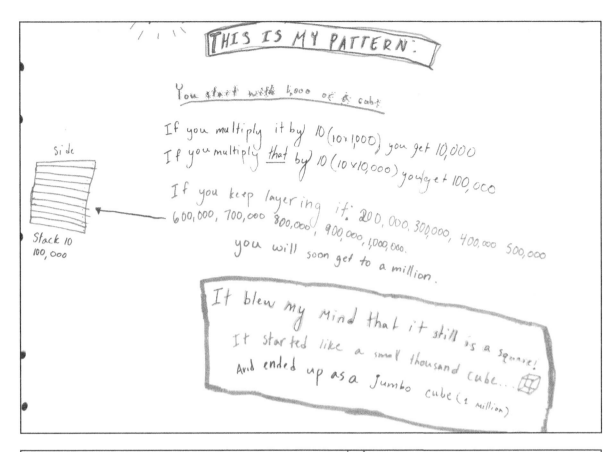

THIS IS MY PATTERN:

You start with 1,000 of a cube

If you multiply it by 10 (10×1,000) you get 10,000
If you multiply _that_ by 10 (10×10,000) you get 100,000

If you keep layering it: 200,000, 300,000, 400,000, 500,000, 600,000, 700,000, 800,000, 900,000, 1,000,000.
you will soon get to a million.

Side

Stack 10
100,000

It blew my mind that it still is a square! It started like a small thousand cube... And ended up as a Jumbo cube (1 million)

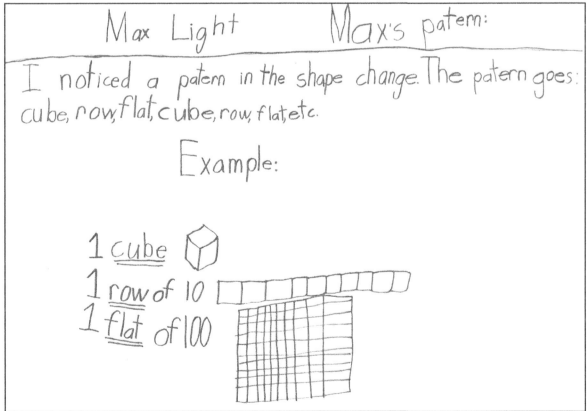

Max Light   Max's patern:

I noticed a patern in the shape change. The patern goes:
cube, row, flat, cube, row, flat, etc.

Example:

1 <u>cube</u>
1 <u>row</u> of 10
1 <u>flat</u> of 100

Figures 8a and 8b. Noticing that the shape repeats in each period.

As you move around, look for openings and possibilities where a conferral could be powerful—where the short moments you have with kids can matter in a big way if you ask the right questions. Sit and confer with students to help the mathematics emerge. For example, note Diana's moves in the conferral box that follows as she supports Tarak and Sydney (Figure 6, shown on p. 19) to consider the associative property.

Inside One Classroom: Conferring with Students at Work

Diana (the teacher): I'm so interested in the strategy that you are working on. May I sit and confer with you?

Sydney: Sure.

Tarak: We figured out that 10 of the large packing boxes would make a big long box and that it holds 10,000 cubes.

Diana: This is so interesting. That is what I thought I heard you say before, and that's why I wanted to sit and confer with you. How many cubes fit in the packing box?

Tarak: 1,000. See, it is 10 pallets and each pallet is a 10x10, and that's 100, so altogether it's 10x100.

Diana: So, are you saying that 10 of these thousands equal 10,000? Is it ok if I write this down on your paper to make sure I understand clearly what you are saying? *(Both Tarak and Sydney nod affirmatively.)* If I write something that is not what you mean, though, you tell me, ok? *(Diana writes "10 x (10x10x10) = 10,000.")* I put parentheses around 10x10x10 because that is the part about the thousand–the packing box—that you did first. Mathematicians use parentheses like this to help their audience know what part they did first. So, this is 10,000. How many pallets would that be?

Sydney: Well, I know that there are 10 pallets in the large cube, so if there are 10 large cubes in a big long box, then there would be 100 pallets.

Tarak: Yeah, there are 100 hundreds.

Diana: Wow! That's interesting, isn't it? Let me write that, too. *(Diana writes "100x100 = 10x1000.")* Is this true? *(Both students are now quiet, puzzled and pondering the question.)*

Sydney: Look! We just took a zero from one number and moved it to the other.

Diana: Say more about that.

Author's notes

As Diana confers, notice how she starts the conferral by listening and getting clarification.

Two equivalent expressions are now on the table for consideration. This can become a big moment if Diana can get them to consider the equivalence. She restates what was just said to focus the discussion and she even writes it down, introducing the parentheses very naturally.

Note how Diana makes use of the context. She talks about pallets and packing boxes, not about 100s and 1,000s. This is to help students picture the amounts.

Diana writes an equation to represent what has just been said. She is modeling what a mathematician does.

Diana asks for more clarification. Encouraging Sydney to talk about what she has noticed will engender even deeper thinking and reflection.

Sydney: It's like one of the zeros in the 100 moved over there to make 1,000.

Diana: What do you think, Tarak?

Tarak: I think she is right, but I don't know why.

Diana: And as mathematicians we want to know why, right? *(Diana smiles, modeling how mathematicians look for structure and regularity and need to justify their statements.)* Let me write more down so we don't forget what we know so far, and let's see if we can figure this out. This is so interesting! Why **do** the zeros move? *(Diana writes: "(10x10) x (10x10) = 10 x (10x10x10).")*

Sydney: Oh... oh! I think I get it! It's just that we are multiplying by 10! The parentheses part is moving!

Tarak: Oh yeah! And I think we could do (10x10x10) x 10, too! There would be 1,000 long boxes. These are all equal to 10,000 cubes!

Diana: Wow! This idea is a big one! Do you think you could make your poster about this idea and find a way to convince the other mathematicians in our community about this?

Diana ensures the conferral includes both students in the thinking. It is so easy to forget that the social interaction is critical. Diana does not forget. In fact, she challenges the pair to figure out the "why" of what Sydney has put forth and models again what mathematicians do.

Now the associative property is emerging.

Diana celebrates what the students have done and explicitly asks them to convince the community of this discovery. A focused poster and argument is far more powerful than a simple restatement of the complete progression of the work.

Math Journals

During the last five minutes of class, ask students to write in their math journals about the big "a-ha" moments or discoveries today.

> *"Before we end for today, write about your latest thinking so that you can hold on to it. What are the big ideas you are working on? I will read what you wrote and write back to you."*

Taking the time to reflect will help them hold on to their ideas, expose areas of confusion, and set the stage for tomorrow's work. Reading these entries will help you, the teacher, see where the students are on the landscape of learning, plan conferrals, and understand what happened for the students you didn't get to confer with today. Before the next class, read the entries and respond to each mathematician with a question or prompt to strengthen or challenge their thinking. Use the strategies and big ideas on the landscape of learning described in the Overview of this unit as a guide. A sample journal entry with Cathy's comments during field testing follows as an illustration.

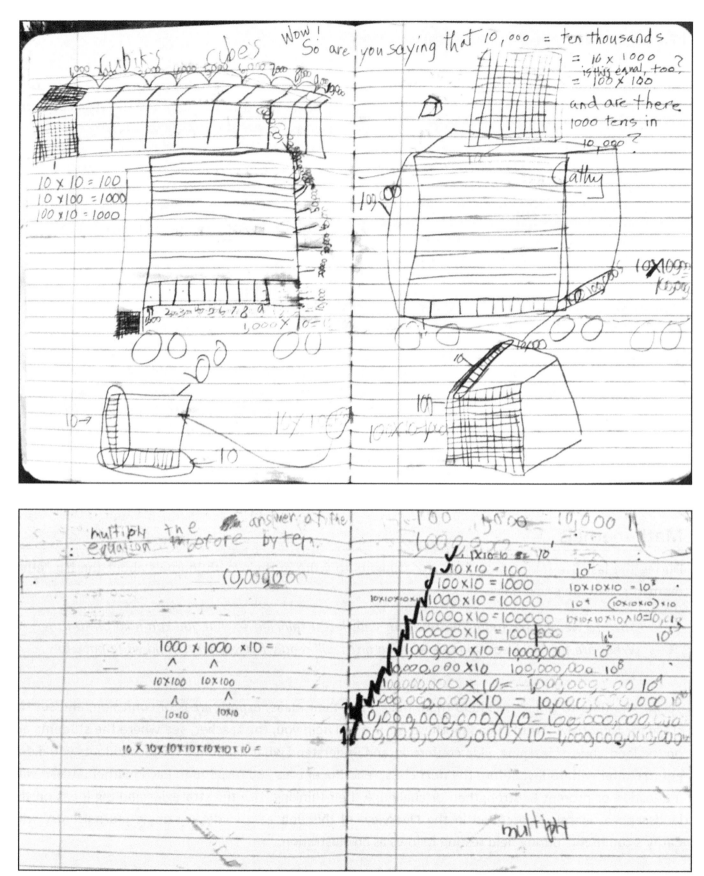

Figure 9. Cathy's comments on a journal entry.

Reflections on the Day

Today students explored what happens when powers of ten are multiplied by another 10. They have likely noticed patterns in the shapes of the boxes, which will have helped them to notice patterns in the number of zeros in the capacity of each box. Take note of the many ideas and strategies you witnessed emerging today and think about the gallery walk and math congress that you will hold tomorrow. Which strategies and ideas would be powerful to develop and prove? How will you support students to write mathematical arguments to justify what they have noticed and the conjectures they offer? Which posters will you use in the congress, and in which order, to ensure a rich, growth-producing conversation for everyone?

DAY TWO

EXAMINING STRUCTURE AND REGULARITY AND CRAFTING PROOFS

Materials Needed

Students' work from Day One

Extra copies of Appendix A to use as needed

Lined sticky notes, several per student

Math Journals

Markers and Pencils

Today begins with students reading their math journals, specifically the comments and entries you made as you reflected on what they wrote at the end of math workshop yesterday. You will be conferring today to help them develop strong justifications for the conjectures they put forth. Then a gallery walk ensues. After the gallery walk, a math congress is held to discuss a few of the ideas and strategies more deeply with emphasis placed on how many cubes each box holds, and on the structure and regularities (the patterns and big ideas) that students noticed when multiplying by 10 repeatedly.

Day Two Outline

Math Journals and Crafting Proofs

❖ Provide quiet time with math journals for students to read comments they received and to revisit their own reflections from the previous day.

❖ Confer with children as they work on their posters, asking them to consider the most important things they want to tell their audience about the structure and regularities they noticed when multiplying by ten, and/or about the shapes of the boxes.

❖ Support them to craft convincing justifications for their conjectures.

Facilitating the Gallery Walk

❖ Conduct a gallery walk to allow students time to reflect and comment on each other's posters.

Facilitating the Math Congress

❖ Convene students at the meeting area to discuss a few important noticings, such as patterns, structure, and regularities they noticed when they examined what each box held.

Math Journals and Crafting Proofs

Provide students about 5-10 minutes to read over your responses to their journal entries from Day One. This time should also prepare them to focus on the writing of viable mathematical arguments. Move around and confer with students as they work. Help them to form conjectures and generalizations about what they have noticed and support them to write strong arguments as justifications. Ask them to consider the most important things they want to tell their audience about the structure and regularities they noticed when they multiplied by 10, or about the shapes of the boxes. Remind them that it is not necessary to write about everything they did, but instead to concentrate on convincing their audience about the important things they discovered and want to defend. The main purpose of a gallery walk is the development of the reading and writing of viable arguments, but it is also to provide time for reflection, refinement, and consolidation of the thinking learners generated as they worked on the investigation. When students are postering, the ideas they write about should go beyond describing what they did, and towards writing about their breakthroughs, new ideas, and insights. Encourage students in this work (rather than emphasizing or requesting that they write about their steps from start to finish). Doing this will support their development toward writing convincing mathematical arguments—proof-making. As you move around conferring and helping your students get ready for the gallery walk, look for moments where you can help them consider the difference between just listing a few examples and putting forth a conjecture and writing a logical argument to prove it.

Facilitating the Gallery Walk

The students' role in the gallery walk is an important one. Their thoughtful consideration of one another's work in this community of mathematicians can help them deepen their own thinking, question the validity of their peers' mathematical arguments, and help to develop new strategies. Spend some time helping students develop language for responding to the posters. Sentence frames such as "I agree with ___ because ___." and "I have a question about ___." are more helpful than brief notes, like "nice job." Emphasize a quiet atmosphere so that all reviewers can read and think before commenting. This time should be taken seriously. Ask students to start at different places and choose three or four posters to focus on, recording their comments on lined sticky notes arranged on a clipboard. Encourage them to spread out so that all posters will have at least a few comments. After about ten minutes, ask them to finish up their final notes and return to their own posters to read the feedback they were given. You can also give students time to revise their work based on the feedback they received.

During the gallery walk it's important that you make comments on posters as well, so that students see you as a member of the community who is really interested in their thinking. Look for moments and places where you can show them you are seriously trying to understand their thinking; and remember, you are their mentor. Appreciate their good thinking, comment on interesting approaches, and suggest where more detail could be helpful to support understanding. Raise questions that might push for generalization. As you move around, look for big ideas and strategies from the landscape that have been justified well. This will help you to plan which pieces of work you will select for the congress if you haven't done that already.

Facilitating the Math Congress

Review the posters and choose a few that you can use for a discussion that will deepen understanding and support growth along the landscape of learning described in the Overview. There is not necessarily one best plan for a congress. There are many different plans that might all be supportive of development. You'll want to make this congress supportive of the development of place value by focusing on the structure and regularities students noticed, such as how the shape of the boxes repeats in each period (but scales up), or the pattern of the zeros. Look for posters that will generate a conversation on the commutative and associative properties to provide discussion justifying the regularities they noticed. If it seems natural to introduce exponents as students talk about multiplying by 10 repeatedly, go for it! It's certainly not a targeted goal in grade 4, but when mathematical moments present themselves, don't hold back! A window into one classroom follows as an example. The work under discussion can be seen in Figure 10.

Inside One Classroom: A Portion of the Math Congress

Diana (the teacher): Ok, we've heard from Hsin-Hua and Bebe *(their work sample is shown in Figure 5)* who convinced us that when you multiply a number by 10, it is the same as having that many tens, and that explains why the zero gets placed at the end. The number moves over a place to show how many tens there are. Nice work! And, then we heard from Tarak and Sydney *(their work sample is shown in Figure 6)* who showed us how the parentheses were just moving around, but the expressions were all equal! Also a nice contribution! Levi and Cole, would you bring up your poster next? There are a few things on it that I think would be interesting to discuss. Start with what you have written on the bottom.

Cole: We noticed that the number of times you multiply by 10, that's how many zeros there would be. This number is big! A zillion or something!! It has 21 zeros, so we know 10 was multiplied by 10 a total of 21 times. When you conferred with us you told us mathematicians wrote it with little numbers up higher.

Levi: Because it is not 21x10. It's 10x10x10... And you keep going... 21 of them. So, we wrote a little 21. And that makes it have 21 zeros.

Diana: Wow! Put your hand up if you understand what Cole and Levi mean. Let's all turn to a partner and help each other understand what they mean. *(After a few minutes of pair talk, Diana resumes whole group discussion.)* Ok, let's come back together and see if we can figure this out. Did anyone have a helpful partner? Tarak?

Author's notes

Diana chooses to start the congress with a discussion on the commutative and associative properties of multiplication and how they explain the regularities that happen when you multiply by ten. This gets right to the heart of place value. A conversation like this will be beneficial for all. But then she goes to a piece that will introduce exponents.

Asking if anyone had a helpful partner implicitly sends the message that pair talk needs to be accountable talk.

Tarak: Sydney and I agree. We think it is just like what we said. It's just ten times, lots of times, and every time you do it another zero goes down. That's also like what Hsin-Hua and Bebe said.

Diana: So, if I write 10x10x10, that is 10 to the 3rd power... that just means that I scaled the box size up ten times, then another ten times, and then another ten times? And so how many cubes are in that box, and what shape is the box? Turn and talk again.

Avni: 10x10x10. It's 1,000. We know that, 3 zeros... and it's cube! I know it. Because it is always a cube before the comma.

Diana: Avni, would you share a little more of what you and Oliver were talking about?

Avni: It's always a cube when it comes before the comma. That's what blew my mind! It's always 3 zeros in between the commas. One million is a cube, too. Because it has 6 zeros. It's 1,000 times bigger than 1,000, so it is a giant cube!

Max: Oh, I get it! That's cool.

Diana: Wow! So many regularities! Patterns and relationships everywhere!! This is what makes math so much fun, isn't it? The regularities we discover!! And, the most fun is in trying to figure out why they are happening.

Diana knows that noticing the patterns that happen when you multiply by ten is on the landscape and ensures that she promotes and supports a conversation on it.

The congress has been instrumental in supporting the community to consider how powerful our place value system is.

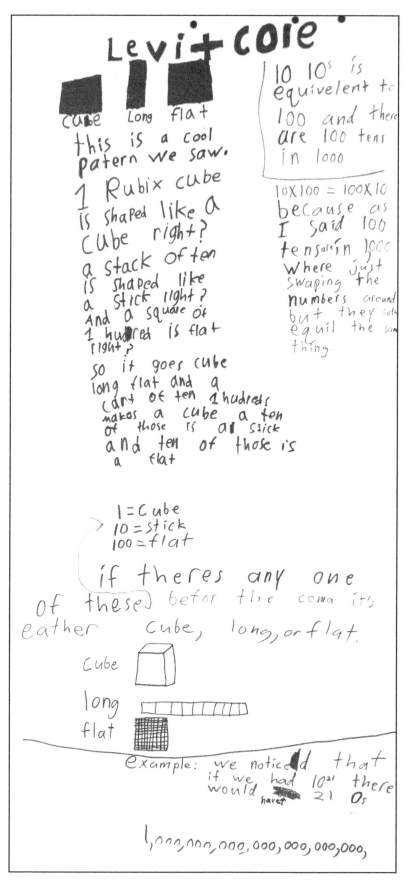

Figure 10. Cole and Levi's poster, discussed during the math congress.

Math Journals

At the end of the congress, provide everyone with some reflective writing time. You might ask students to write about an idea they thought was particularly powerful, a new idea they are now thinking about, or the connections they see between the posters shared. What do they understand about the shapes of the boxes and the numbers of cubes, or the parentheses indicating the associativity of the numbers? Some may be interested in reflecting on the relationship between the number of zeros and the power of 10. Giving students time to articulate their new understandings will also provide you with important information that you can use as formative assessment and that will inform your choice of partnerships for the next investigation.

Reflections on the Day

Math workshop began today with the students looking at the comments they received in their journals, taking the questions and challenges posed, and extending or reinforcing their work. They continued deepening their understanding by refining their own posters and carefully considering the work of their classmates during the gallery walk. The congress helped to solidify and extend everyone's understanding of the structures and regularities of our number system by highlighting the commutative and associative properties and the patterns that emerge when multiplying by ten. Giving children time to review their ideas, to justify their thinking, to extend their thinking to other examples, and to learn from each other's work contributes to the development of these young mathematicians and turns the classroom into a true mathematics laboratory.

DAY THREE

HOW BIG IS A MILLION?

Materials Needed

One each of
1"x1"x1", 2"x2"x2",
and 3"x3"x3" cubes

A measuring tool,
such as a tape
measure or a meter
stick with both
centimeters and
inches

One roll of adding
machine paper

Chart or poster
paper

Math Journals

Markers and Pencils

The day begins with a minilesson designed to focus discussion on using the commutative and associative properties of multiplication to multiply by powers of ten. The ideas explored in the minilesson will serve as a foundation for the underlying big ideas that explain the place value patterns that occur when multiplying by powers of ten. Next, students will put their number sense to work estimating the size of a giant cube of 1,000,000 puzzle cubes, each 3" by 3" by 3", and pondering whether the amount will fit on the back of a delivery truck.

Day Three Outline

Minilesson: A string of related problems

❖ A string of related problems supports students to continue exploring the commutative and associative properties of multiplication and their relationship to the place value patterns that occur when multiplying by powers of ten.

Developing the Context

❖ Remind students about the truckload of cubes in the investigation begun on Day One and how it was a giant cube made of 1,000 shipping boxes.

❖ Send students off in pairs to determine whether such a giant cube would actually fit in a truck. Have everyone investigate with a 3"x3"x3" cube first, and then suggest they explore other smaller sizes once they have determined that the truck would have to be so large it would require at least two lanes and not be allowed on the road!

Supporting the Investigation

❖ As students work, encourage them to estimate the dimensions of the giant cube comprised of 1 million puzzle cubes.

❖ Note the strategies students use and confer with a few groups as they work.

Minilesson: A String of Related Problems

Work through each problem one at a time, inviting students to share their strategies. Use the open array to represent students' thinking where appropriate, but also write equations when students start noting and discussing the relationships between the problems. Use the equations to represent how factors can be regrouped and invite discussion on how these ideas connect to the ideas about powers of ten discussed on Day Two.

The String:

10 x 3

3 x 10

100 x 3

10 x 30

100 x 100

100 x 300

Behind the Numbers

This string has been carefully constructed to support learners' understanding of how the commutative and associative properties of multiplication can be helpful when multiplying by powers of ten. The first two problems immediately bring up the commutative property. This is purposeful, as it provides an opportunity to discuss why the 3 bumps over to the tens column and a 0 is placed in the units column: 10x3 = 3x10; if there are 3 tens, the 3 moves over to the tens column. The next two problems support a consideration of both the commutative and associative properties: 100x3 = (10x10) x 3 = (10) x (10x3) = 10x30 = 30x10. As the string continues, students are likely to note many other examples of the commutative and the associative properties of multiplication, as well as the patterns that occur when multiplying by powers of ten: $100 \times 100 = 10 \times 10 \times 10 \times 10 = 10^4 = 10,000$. See if students are able to imagine the shape: there are 10 thousands, and since the thousand is a cube, 10 of them make a large, long box. This associativity can now be extended to larger numbers such as 100x300, or (10x10) x 3 x (10x10) = 30,000. Now there are 3 large, long boxes: 3×10^4.

Inside One Classroom: A Portion of the Minilesson

Diana (the teacher): So, let's start with this one. *(She writes "10x3" on the board.)* Show me with a "thumbs up" when you have had enough time to think. Nora?

Nora: It's 30.

Diana: How did you get 30?

Nora: That's like what we talked about yesterday on a poster. It's the same as 3 tens.

Diana: So, I hear you saying we can think of 10 threes as 3 tens. *(She writes "10x3 = 3x10.")* And either way we look at it will give the same result? (*She draws a 10x3 array and supports students to see that if rotated 90 degrees it becomes a 3x10 array.*) Now, what about this one? *(She writes "100x3" on the board.)* Tarak?

Author's notes

Diana is reiterating what Nora is saying to help the children understand the commutative property. She seeks another example from Tarak so they will see that it is true for these numbers as well.

Tarak: It's 300. I did it the same way as the first one. I know 3 x 100 is 300, so 100 x 3 is 300.

Diana: So, looking at the expression either way is powerful, isn't it? Mathematicians have a name for this. They call it the commutative property because the numbers can be commuted back and forth, like how I commute back and forth to work! Maybe later we can put that up on our strategy wall.

Ready for the next one? *(She writes "10x30.")* Turn and talk to a partner about this one and see if the partner did it the same way you did, or if they used another way. *(She provides pair talk for a few minutes and then resumes.)* Sydney?

Sydney: It's still 300! I can do 30 tens by just adding a zero on the end.

Diana: Can we talk about what you mean by adding a zero, because 30+0 would still be 30, right?

Sydney: Well, 30 is like 30 ones or 3 tens, but if you want 30 tens, everything has to bump over. When you multiply by 10, everything moves over. *(Diana models with an array what Sydney says.)*

Diana: Did anyone think of 10x30 another way? Levi?

Levi: Well, a minute ago we said 30 was 10x3, so 10x10 is a hundred and 3x100 is 300.

Diana: Let me write down what you said. We can say 10 x (10x3) = (10x10) x 3 and I'll put parentheses around the parts you are talking about so we can see what you mean. Mathematicians use parentheses like this to show their audience which parts were done first.

Sydney can see that the "zero trick" is because of the commutativity: 10x30 =30x10. Writing the equation and drawing the array and turning it (rather than only writing the answer) provides a more powerful modeling of the big ideas underlying the place value patterns that occur when multiplying by powers of ten.

Levi is beginning to see the associative property: that 10x30 is the same as (10x10)x3, which can also be expressed as 10x(10x3).

Developing the Context

Remind everyone about the challenge question at the end of Appendix A. Will this giant cube made up of 1,000,000 puzzle cubes really fit in a truck? Is this plausible? Explain that puzzle cubes do come in many sizes and show several: a 1"x1"x1", 2"x2"x2", and a 3"x3"x3". Since we don't know what size cubes the factory had in the box, ask students to begin by investigating the standard size (3"x3"x3") and send them off in pairs to work. When they have finished working on the standard size, invite them to continue with the other sizes.

Teacher Note

Note that the dimensions of the truck have never been given as they are not necessary. **Do not provide measurements of the truck. If a student asks to look up average dimensions of trucks on the internet, ask if that information is necessary.** The context is planned purposefully to provide students with opportunities to imagine large amounts and distances and to estimate with them. Since each cube is 3" wide, the width of the truck would need to be at least 100 x 3" or 300", which equals 25 feet (approximately 7.5 meters). A truck that wide would not even fit in the lane of traffic! Most large cargo trucks are around 10 feet (approximately 3 meters) wide. Semi-trailer trucks can carry large capacities, but only because the length of the bed is much larger than the width, and there can be more than one trailer. The point of this investigation is the reasoning that students do as they work to imagine such a large load. If students suggest researching dimensions of semi-tractor trailers and they want to imagine the 1,000,000 cubes rearranged into a shape other than the cube, let them. Some nice learning can occur. They will also have some fun imagining how big a truck would have to be to hold one million 5"x5"x5" cubes! Others may say that if the 3"x3"x3" is too large a load then anything bigger, such as the 4"x4"x4" or the 5"x5"x5", would be too large also. This type of reasoning is to be encouraged. Even the 2"x2"x2" is likely too large, as 100 of these would take up 200" in width, and 200/12 = 100/6 = 50/3, or approximately 16 feet (almost 5 meters). A very small cube of 1"x1"x1" could work, as the width would be 100", or approximately 7 feet. A teeny cube of 1cm x 1cm x 1cm would easily fit. The giant cube holding 1,000,000 of these cubes would only be 1 cubic meter.

Supporting the Investigation

Move around the room as students work, listening and noting the strategies they are using. Then, as always, sit and confer with a few pairs. Some students may have investigated the total size of the cubes already if they worked quickly through the investigation on Days One and Two. If so, have them make a poster of their strategy, write a justification for their determination, and then invite them to consider the other sizes. Some descriptions of what you might see are provided to help you anticipate what your children might do.

❖ Some students may start by figuring out the dimensions of boxes, pallets and cubes. As you confer, you might ask them if they need to know the dimensions of all the boxes to imagine the dimensions of the giant box that holds 1,000,000 cubes. Stay grounded in the context, encouraging them to imagine the giant cube in the truck and wonder aloud with them what the dimensions of that cube would be. You might encourage the drawing of a line to represent the first dimension and mark the length of one 3" cube on it to get them started. See Figure 11.

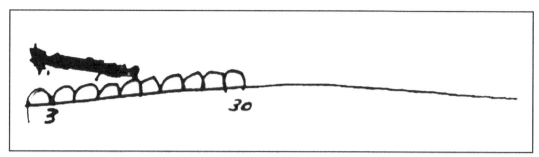

Figure 11. Modeling 10 cubes along the width of the bed of the truck.

❖ Others may work only with one dimension, such as the width as well, but explain that the other dimensions will be the same length since the shape is a cube. Celebrate this insight and point out that by imagining the width of the massive cube, they could figure out how wide the truck would have to be to hold it. Once they have a number for the width, they can decide if that size is plausible for a truck going down the road. As they work on one dimension you will likely see a variety of computation strategies. Some students may begin by drawing a line and skip counting by 3s as they know that the cube measures 3"x3"x3". Others may use a double number line, marking off the 3s, but also marking ten 3s as the width of one pallet. Remind them of the minilesson and ask if they "just know" 10 times 3, or 100 times 3. See Figure 12.

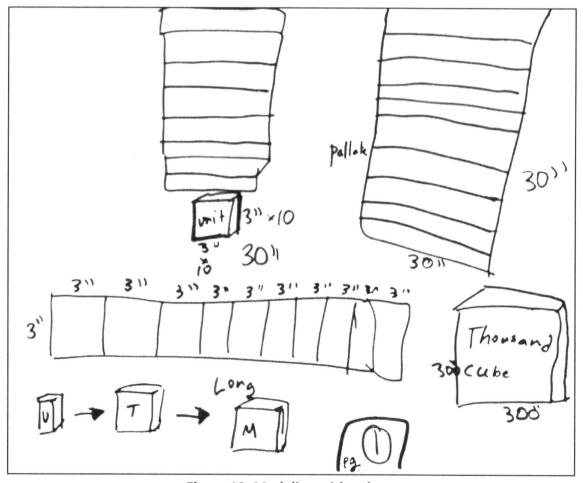

Figure 12. Modeling with cubes.

❖ Some students may figure out the dimensions quickly given the strategies used in the minilesson, for example using 100x3. Once they figure out that the massive cube holding 1,000,000 puzzle cubes measures 300 inches on a side, they will likely want to figure out how many feet that is to help them imagine the size better. Dividing 300 by 12 may be a challenge to some, but the task has a low floor; even tedious strategies (like repeated addition or subtraction of 12s) can work. Ask if they know 10x12 and then support the use of partial quotients: 120/12 + 120/12 + 60/12 = 25. Use the open number line to model this as shown in Figure 13 below. The open array is not a good model to use here as the 300 is a linear measurement, not an area measurement.

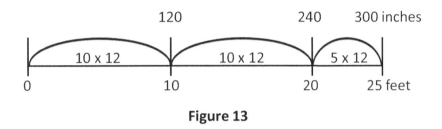

Figure 13

❖ Depending on the amount of work you have done previously with strings of related problems (like those in the minilesson resource *Extending Multiplication and Division*), you may see some students solving 300/12 by simplifying it to 100/4. The minilesson on Day Four is designed to bring this strategy forth for discussion.

Once students determine that the length of the bed of the truck would need to be 25 feet, encourage them to consider how long this is. Provide them with a roll of adding machine paper or a measuring tool (such as a yardstick, meter stick, or tape measure) and encourage them to measure out 25 feet to see how long it is. Alternatively, they might estimate how many yards this length is by dividing 25 by 3. Encourage estimation, such as using 24÷3 to find a length of a bit more than 8 yards. Of course, if the package is a cube then the width will have to be equal to the length. Ask students to consider if a truck this wide could drive in a lane on the thruway, or on city streets. This is a terrific opportunity to allow the children to mathematize their lived experience. Allow for many ideas and entry points to maintain a truly investigative atmosphere, including searching the internet for street widths and/or dimensions of trucks. These real-world examples bring energy to the math classroom as the children see how mathematics is used in the world.

Teacher Note

Once students have finished determining whether a giant cube of one million 3"x3"x3" cubes will fit in the truck, they can consider whether other sizes of cubes would fit. What if we were shipping 1,000,000 2"x2"x2" cubes? Would they fit? What about tiny 1"x1"x1" keychain cubes? Would a giant cube of a million of those tiny cubes fit in a truck? This work can extend into the next day's lesson, as the congress will not be held until Day Four.

Inside One Classroom: Conferring with Students at Work

Diana (the teacher): I've been watching what you two are doing and it looks like such an interesting strategy. Can I sit and confer with you? *(The students have drawn an outline of a giant box and are marking the bottom line off in segments and writing "3" above each segment.)*

Zeke: We are trying to figure out how big the giant cube will be. We know each cube is 3 inches. *(He gets to 30.)* That's 10 cubes.

Alana: That's a shipping box.

Diana: So, you're marking off each cube. That sounds like a lot of work!

Zeke: Yes, it is, but we wanted to be sure.

Alana: How many shipping boxes do we need?

Diana: What are you thinking, Alana? How will that help you? *(Both students are silent.)* Hmm.

Alana: Well, we've got 1 shipping box, and that's 30 inches. So, 2 would be 60 inches.

Diana: *(After some wait time)* Can you see what she's saying, Zeke?

Zeke: Doubling? That's a good idea.

Diana: Could you take it even further? Alana, you were asking how many shipping boxes you need. What do you think?

Alana: We need 10. We figured that out before. So it's ten 30's. That's 10x30.

Zeke: That's 300! So it's 300 inches.

Diana: Are you sure?

Zeke: Yes! Because earlier we figured out that the giant cube was 10 shipping boxes across, so it's definitely right!

Diana: That's terrific. Could you make a poster that shows the class what you figured out?

Alana: Well, the shipping box was 3x10, and 10 of them... I think it would be 3x10x10.

Zeke: 300 inches! Whoa! That's a lot!

Author's notes

Note how Diana listens first before she sits down. She then explains what she thinks the pair is doing and asks for clarification. Once she is sure of their strategy she will be able to better support them. The intent is not to lead them to a strategy she may know or to an answer, but to support them as young mathematicians.

Notice how Diana encourages the two students to help each other.

The pair began with an additive strategy, which they may have been using because it came to them quickly. But to a mathematician, efficiency is important. Alana has noticed the relationship between the shipping box, which is 10 cubes wide, and the giant cube, which is 10 of those, but wasn't sure at first how to use this information.

With a little bit of questioning from Diana, Alana was able to see that the width of the giant cube was 10 times longer than the width of the shipping box, and what they were actually doing was using the associative property for multiplication: (3x10)x10, or 3x(10x10), or 3x100. These are big ideas for these young mathematicians and Diana leaves them to allow them sufficient think time to work through their thinking.

As students begin to reach conclusions about the size of the giant cube, ask them to prepare posters presenting their findings for a gallery walk and congress on Day Four. Explain that mathematicians often want to share their findings with each other, and that when they do they are careful to choose the most important ideas to share. As students prepare their work on poster paper, they should not copy or explain every step they took. Instead, encourage students to record how their thinking changed, the interesting connections they noticed, and the arguments they might use to convince each other that their answers are correct.

Reflections on the Day

Today your students had the opportunity to examine how the commutative and associative properties can be helpful when multiplying. In the minilesson they explored how 100x3=10x30, and how 100x300 can be expressed as 3x100x100. Later, as they worked to determine the lengths of the sides of the giant cube of 1 million puzzle cubes, they discovered that 100 threes can be grouped as 10 groups of 3x10. In figuring out whether the cube would fit on a truck, they likely considered how many feet were in 300 inches and several strategies for division computation may have come up, such as partial quotients and simplifying. Note the division strategies students are using as this provides you with important information to inform your choices as you do further minilessons with your group over the course of the next few weeks. As they worked today, you also had opportunities to see the types of estimation strategies your students are using. Estimation is not just about rounding; it is about making sense of the problem at hand and making wise choices about numbers that might make the calculation easier. The investigation also provided opportunities for your students to make important connections between measurement and number, deepening their understanding of number relations. Celebrate their noticings and how they justify their thinking. Remember to reflect on what you see each day, on the big ideas being constructed and on the strategies that you see being used. Document the growth you see on the landscape. If you are using the New Perspectives assessment app, take a short video clip and a picture of children's work and add it to the landscape.

DAY FOUR

WILL IT FIT IN THE TRUCK?

Materials Needed

Students' work from Day Three

Lined Sticky Notes, four to six per student

One each of 1"x1"x1", 2"x2"x2", and 3"x3"x3" cubes

A measuring tool, such as a tape measure or a meter stick with both centimeters and inches

One roll of adding machine paper

Math Journals

Markers and Pencils

Today begins with a minilesson, a string of related problems designed to support the development of division strategies. After the minilesson, students add finishing touches to their posters from Day Three and prepare for a gallery walk, noticing and wondering about other students' work and comparing it to their own. After the gallery walk, a math congress is held to discuss a few of the emerging ideas about multiplication and measurement more deeply. The day ends with journal writing.

Day Four Outline

Minilesson: A String of Related Problems
❖ Work on a string of related problems to encourage discussion on simplification as a strategy for division.

Facilitating the Gallery Walk
❖ Confer with children as they put finishing touches on their posters, asking them to consider the most important things they want to tell their audience.
❖ Conduct a gallery walk to allow students time to reflect and comment on each other's posters.

Facilitating the Math Congress
❖ Convene students at the meeting area to discuss a few important ideas that have surfaced in their work.

Math Journals
❖ At the end of the congress, provide everyone with some reflective writing time.

Minilesson: A String of Related Problems

As you did on Day Three, work through each problem one at a time, inviting students to share their strategies. Use the open number line to represent students' thinking where appropriate, as it more closely represents the context of the cubes in the truck that they have been investigating than the array. Also write equations when students start noting and discussing the relationships between the problems. Use the equations to represent how equivalent factors can be eliminated from the dividend and the divisor to produce equivalent expressions that may be easier to compute.

The String:

100 / 4

200 / 4

200 / 8

400 / 16

800 / 32

300 / 12

Behind the Numbers

This string has been carefully constructed to support learners' understanding of how division problems can be simplified when the dividend and divisor have common factors. Using simplification can often make a division problem so much easier to compute that it can be done mentally. The first problem is a "helper." It is assumed to be an easy problem as most students will likely use their knowledge of money. The second and third problems provide opportunities for students to examine what happens when the dividend doubles, but the divisor remains the same, and the reciprocal case of when the dividend remains the same, but the divisor doubles. Students may notice after they have solved the third problem that the quotient is the same as the quotient of the first problem. If not, it doesn't matter because the next two problems will also have the same quotients. The last problem is simplified by pulling a factor of 3 from the dividend and the divisor, effectively setting up two equivalent expressions again: 300/12 = 100/4. Note that the numbers in this last problem are the same as the numbers in the investigation if students have used a strategy of figuring out how many feet there are in the width (or height or length) of the giant cube. One hundred 3"x3"x3" cubes result in a dimension of 300" along the width of the bed of the truck. When determining how many feet this is, students will have some computation to do: 300/12. Providing the minilesson at this point is purposeful. You may find that some of your students notice this connection as they prepare posters for the gallery walk and congress, but others may not. Either way, it will be an interesting point to discuss in the congress.

Inside One Classroom: A Portion of the Minilesson

Diana (the teacher): So, let's start with this one. *(She writes 100/4 on the board.)* It might help if you think about money. Show me with a "thumbs up" when you have had enough time to think. Hsin-Hua?

Hsin-Hua: I think it's 25. Because 25+25=50, and 50+50=100, and I know there are four 25s in 100.

Tarak: I agree. It's 25. I know that 25x2=50 and 50x2=100.

Nora: I know 4 quarters is $1.00, so 4x25=100.

Diana: I hear all of you saying we can break 100 into 4 parts, and each part will be 25 units long? Give me a "thumbs up" if you agree, or a thumb to the side if you're not so sure. *(All thumbs go up so Diana goes on.)* Now, what about this one? *(She writes "200/4" on the board and provides some think time before starting discussion)* Wyn?

Wyn: It's 50. I cut 200 in half and that's 100, and then I cut 100 in half and that's 50 and there are 4 of them.

Diana: That's interesting, Wyn. You still have 4 parts, but they're bigger. Why do you think that is?

Wyn: Because the number line is twice as long; 200 is twice 100.

Diana: The number we're breaking up, or the dividend, is twice as big and we cut it into the same number of parts—the divisor stayed the same. So, you are saying the length of the parts—the quotient—will now be twice as long? Let's turn and talk about this. If we double the dividend but keep the divisor the same, will we always have a quotient that has doubled?

Bebe: I noticed something! Wyn is right. 25x4=100, and 50x4=200! We have four 25s and four 50s.

Diana: Wow, Bebe. Nice noticing. We still have 4 parts, but the size of the parts has doubled so the product has doubled? We need to get your strategy up on our strategy wall, Wyn. That's a nice relationship that you noticed.

Author's notes

Diana starts the string off with a "helper"—an easy problem that will become a helper for more challenging problems as the string progresses.

Diana writes the 50 in the middle of the number line and shows 4 jumps, marking 25 each time.

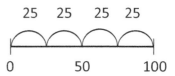

Diana draws a second line underneath, extending it to be twice as long as the first. By leaving both lines and the parts visibly proportional, she provides a model for students to consider how the problems are related.

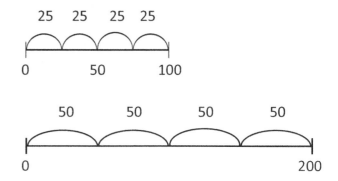

Diana provides time for her students to consider this idea. She wants to push her students to generalize the arithmetic and to consider relations, not to just do a procedure to get an answer.

Diana: I have another problem in mind. *(She writes "200/8" and provides pair talk for a few minutes and then resumes.)* Sydney?

Sydney: It's 25 again. This time you doubled the divisor, so we have twice as many parts. Now the parts are half as long as before because each part was cut in half. It's 25 again.

Diana: Oliver?

Oliver: I agree but I thought about it in a different way. There's 4 for each 100, so 8 lines will be 200. That's still 25.

Diana: Hmmm… Oliver, are you seeing a connection between the first problem and this one? Are you thinking that 100, the dividend, was doubled and 4, the divisor, was doubled so the quotients will be the same? Are you saying 100/4 = 200/8? Everyone, turn and talk about this. Is Oliver right? Because if he is, this might be a really important, and helpful, idea. And as you talk, consider this one, too *(she writes "400/16")*.

Levi: It's 25! If you keep doubling both numbers, it will always be 25.

Diana: Really? Is that true?

Luca: It's like if I have 100 cookies, and 4 people, we each get 25. If I have 200 cookies, and 8 people we still get 25. If we have 400 cookies and 16 people, I would still get 25.

Diana: This is so cool! Let me write down what you're saying. This sounds like it should go on our strategy wall. If we double the number we're breaking up, which is called the dividend, and we double the divisor, which is the number of parts we're breaking it into, then our answer will always be the same? That would be so useful if it's true! For example, would it help with these? *(She writes "800/32" and "300/12.")* Turn and talk.

Cole: Oh my gosh! I think I see something! I don't think it's just doubling! I think as long as you do the same thing to both numbers it works. 100x8=800 and 4x8=32; and 100x3=300 and 4x3=12. The answer to these is 25, too!

Diana posts student strategies throughout the year on a large wall. When strategies are generalized and justified, they are named for the mathematician who put them forth and they become part of the mathematical culture Diana is developing.

The idea that scaling in tandem and/or simplifying produces an equivalent expression that can be substituted or exchanged for another is huge. This is an important strategy on the division landscape. Scaling up and down can often produce equivalent expressions that can easily be solved mentally.

Pair talk is a very critical move here. Using it strategically when a big idea is on the horizon provides the needed reflection time to consider justifications.

Facilitating the Gallery Walk

Ask students to return to the posters they began on Day Three, adding any finishing touches they desire. As they work, move around and confer, asking them to consider the most important things they want to tell their audience and how they will convince them. Look for ways to take their understanding to a deeper level or to justify generalizations of big ideas that emerged. As the teacher, you are a mentor. But, you are also a member of the audience. Asking questions will help students clarify their ideas. For example, you might try out questions like these: "What do you want me to understand about what you found out?" "How do you think your fellow mathematicians will make sense of your ideas?"

Remind students that it is not necessary to write about everything they did. The posters are not necessarily explanations of everything that was done (including false starts, mistakes, and changes made), but instead are justifications of steps for a complete solution, or justifications of conjectures and insights. You are providing students with an important opportunity to review and refine their thinking—to read and write a viable mathematical argument. This is one of the standards of mathematical practice and another purpose of the gallery walk.

Once students have posted their work, remind them that gallery walks should be quiet times so that all mathematicians can read and think before commenting. This time should be taken seriously. Distribute the sticky notes to students and take some yourself as well. During the gallery walk it's important for you to look at all the pieces for big ideas and strategies from the landscape, so you can plan which pieces of work you will select for the congress.

Facilitating the Math Congress

Review the posters and choose a few that you can use for a discussion that will deepen understanding and support growth along the landscape of learning described in the Overview. For example, notice if students realize there will be 100 cubes along each dimension of the giant cube. Do they realize that 100x100x100=1,000,000? Can they easily multiply by 100, realizing that 100x3=3x100? Do any students make use of exponents, remembering the conversation that likely happened in the math congress on Day Two? Do they realize that the 3"x3"x3" cube produces dimensions of 300 inches; that a 2"x2"x2" cube produces dimensions of 200 inches; and, the 1"x1"x1" cube produces dimensions of 100 inches? When converting inches into feet, have any students made use of 300/12=100/4 from the minilesson and consequently realized that 25 feet is way too wide for a truck that needs to drive down the road? Did you see any other evidence of helpful division strategies as the children figured out how many feet wide the cube must be? Have any students used the commutative and associative properties? Some may have deepened their understanding of the shapes of numbers, noticing that because of the cube's equal side lengths, they only needed to figure out one dimension in order to see if the cube would fit in the truck. Look at students' work with an eye to the big ideas and strategies on the landscape and you will see the potential for many rich discussions.

Math Journals

At the end of the congress, provide everyone with some reflective writing time. Questions you might ask students to address are:

❖ Did you hear about an idea in math workshop that you thought was interesting or particularly powerful?

❖ Is there a new idea that you are now thinking about? How will you start investigating it?

Reflections on the Day

Today your students had the opportunity to further deepen their understanding of large numbers. On Days One and Two they explored the place value patterns that occur when an amount is multiplied by a power of ten. They also worked to envision 1,000,000 as a giant cube, or as 10x(10x10x10x10x10), or as (10x10)x(10x10x10x10) and examined how the commutative and associative properties were involved in the place value patterns that occurred. On Day Three and today, students had another opportunity to envision 1,000,000 by imagining a truck with a million cubes—an amount so large the truck would not be able to go down the road! Even one million of the 1"x1"x1" cubes is too large an amount unless the cubes are unpackaged and rearranged and the truck has a non-square bed! Students also examined relationships and strategies for computation that could be helpful when dividing, such as partial quotients and simplifying, and they explored a case when these strategies were helpful for estimating as they considered how many feet were in 300 inches. The investigation also provided opportunities for your students to make important connections between measurement and number, deepening their understanding of number relations.

Today you also had another chance to look at your students' work and get a better idea of where each student is travelling on the landscape of learning. Remember to track each student's mathematical development on individual landscapes!

DAY FIVE

PACKAGING AND SHIPPING COMPANIES

Materials Needed

Quick Image cards (Appendix E)

Envelopes (one for each student with a strip cut from an appropriate company sheet on Appendix D)

Inventory Recording Sheet (Appendix B, one per student)

Total Company Inventory Sheet (Appendix C, one per group)

Thin loose-leaf binders or folders, one for each company

Three-prong hole puncher

Handheld calculators, one for each company

Today begins with a minilesson using a string of quick images from Appendix E to support the development of addition regrouping strategies, the basis of the standard addition algorithm. Students then form companies, name them, and engage in taking inventory of the cubes they have in their warehouses.

Day Five Outline

Minilesson: Quick Images

❖ Work on a string of quick images designed to encourage the use of place value and regrouping when adding.

Developing the Context

❖ Explain that over the next several days the class will engage in a simulation game. Today, in preparation, the companies will be formed and named, and an inventory will be taken of the cubes in their warehouse for the start of the game. Each student employee totals up a section of the warehouse and records the total on Appendix B.

❖ Students then determine the total number of cubes in their warehouse, reorganize the warehouse by packing more efficiently, and calculate the dollar value of their supply.

Supporting the Investigation

❖ Note students' strategies as they work and encourage them to consider the equivalence in the numbers as they unpack and pack amounts into new boxes.

Facilitating the Math Congress

❖ Conduct a math congress discussion to highlight more efficient computation strategies.

Minilesson: A String of Related Problems

Using the cards from Appendix E, make the amounts of each problem visible for a few seconds. Place the cards one on top of the other and ask students to determine how many units there are all together. It is helpful to provide small whiteboards or paper and markers for this.

The String

321 + 33

239 + 101

1,042 + 63

1,043 + 168

1,243 + 968

Behind the Numbers

The numbers have been chosen carefully to support students to add like powers of 10 (similar box sizes). The first problem makes use of easily-subitizable groups. Most students will likely add similar boxes for a total of 3 pallets, 5 longs, and 4 loose and report 354. Ensure that all students understand the value of each box and know why it is okay to do this. The second problem requires regrouping: the single 1, when added to the 9 singles, produces a full box of 10, making the 3 longs into 4. The next problem requires regrouping of the longs into one pallet, and the final two problems also require more regrouping.

Developing the Context

Inform students that over the next several days they will be involved in a simulation game. Today, in preparation, they will form companies, name them, take inventory of how many cubes they have in their warehouse, and calculate the dollar value of the inventory. The number of cubes and the value of this inventory will be recorded in their company's ledger, and the cubes will be repacked efficiently (filling each of the larger-size boxes first to get their warehouses organized in preparation for play). Over the course of the next week, each company will be involved in the buying and selling of toy cubes and the replenishing of their inventory.

Have students form groups (approximately four students in each). If the number of students in your class does not allow for groups of four, materials are also provided for groups of three or five. You can mix group sizes as needed to work best for your class of students. Pass out the binders (one to each company) and envelopes with the amounts of cubes to be totaled (one strip from Appendix D to each student). **Ensure that you use the company sheet for the correct group size and provide the students in each group with all the rows from the same company sheet—one each—as otherwise the numbers will not total correctly. Do not mix the strips.** Explain that the warehouses are divided into one section for each employee. Each employee is responsible for determining the total number of cubes in his or her designated station. The three numbers in the envelope are amounts that must be added to determine the total number of cubes in each employee's section. Have students show their work on Appendix B.

After determining the total number of cubes in their sections, students will repack them into appropriate shipping boxes, if necessary, so that cubes are ready to be shipped. Then students record the total number of each type of box into the company ledger and initial them as evidence that they did the inventory and that the total is correct. All members of the company as individuals or pairs should then calculate the complete total inventory of cubes in the warehouse and its value in dollars (cubes sell for $10 each). They then check each other's work for agreement and accuracy and record their totals in the ledger on Appendix C.

Teacher Note

The context allows students to expand their strategies for addition and subtraction to numbers in the tens of thousands and beyond, and to deal with packing and unpacking equivalent amounts. The starting amount at each warehouse is set at 100,000 cubes for each company, although the students will not know this at the beginning as the amounts on their strips are different. For example, four students might have named their company TWIST ITS. Employee A's three sections might total 23,472; Employee B's total might be 24,043; Employee C's total might be 28,080; and Employee D's total might be 24,405. (Note that these are the sums of each of the rows on the grid for a company of four.) The total inventory of the TWIST IT'S warehouse is the sum of these four numbers, or 100,000. Since cubes sell for $10 apiece, the value of the inventory is $1,000,000. All companies will be starting the game with the same amount of inventory, but don't tell them this ahead of time! Some may make computation errors and unequal amounts will provide an incentive to check. The purpose of the calculators is to ensure there is a check on the arithmetic and as an encouragement for students to find their errors and fix them when their totals are not in agreement with the calculator's. During the next week, as the game continues, the employees will be filling orders, replenishing their inventory, packing and unpacking the inventory, and recording the addition and subtraction in their accounting ledgers. At various points, students will also figure out the value of their company's current inventory at $10 per cube.

Supporting the Investigation

As you walk around supporting and conferring with students, note the strategies they are using for the addition. Appendix B is intentionally designed in the form of a place value chart to support students to make use of place value and to suggest packing and unpacking boxes as needed to organize their section of the warehouse into full boxes ready for shipping. Here are some strategies you can anticipate:

❖ Unpacking everything (translating the worth of each box into unit cubes), thereby using an expanded notation (splitting) strategy. For example: 1 shipping box, 3 pallets, 2 longs, and 9 loose cubes would first be written as 1,000 + 300 + 20 + 9. This splitting strategy may be used for each of the three amounts and then the amounts would be added in partial sums, repacked into boxes, and lastly regrouped optimally into full boxes to organize the warehouse and prepare for shipping. This is an example of a splitting strategy, which you will find described in the Overview and depicted on the landscape. As you confer, encourage these students to consider whether all that work is really needed. Perhaps ask if they might just add the totals of the boxes, or whether they think this strategy might change the amount. Try to determine if these students understand the big ideas of equivalence and that place matters (see the Overview). A dialogue box of a conferral with a pair using this strategy is provided for consideration.

❖ Totaling boxes of each type, but in a random order, and repacking everything at the end to organize the cubes into full boxes for shipping. This is an example of regrouping inefficiently, also described in the Overview and depicted on the landscape. As you confer, compliment students on how they are making use of the values of the boxes and just adding these without needing to unpack everything. But then invite them to consider if it would save time to fill complete boxes first and then add.

❖ Starting with the largest boxes first, for example adding up the shipping boxes first, then the pallets, longs, and loose cubes. Once done, these students will need to repack everything again to organize cubes into full boxes for shipping. This is another example of regrouping inefficiently. (See Figure 2 in the Overview.) As you confer with these groups, invite consideration of whether it might be more efficient to start with the loose cubes and fill complete boxes as they add (introducing the algorithm).

❖ Starting with the loose cubes and filling the longs first, then the pallets, then the shipping boxes, and continuing in this manner of regrouping to make the next larger packing shape (multiple of ten). This is an example of using the addition algorithm flexibly and efficiently. The beauty of the algorithm is that little paper is needed as the regrouping is done at the same time as the addition of the boxes. And, of course, this procedure is what underlies the use of the algorithm and why, before the advent of calculators, the abacus and algorithms were the primary tools for accounting.

Inside One Classroom: Conferring with Students at Work

Diana (the teacher): I'm so interested in the strategy that you are working on. May I sit and confer with you?

Jared: Sure.

Tanisha: We wrote down how many cubes are in the boxes. Each shipping box has 1,000 cubes; each pallet has 100; and each long box has 10. Then we added all our numbers up.

Diana: Wow! This is great that you know how many cubes are in each box and I understand why you are adding the amounts all up—to get the total, right?

Jared: Yep. That's it.

Diana: So, that was a lot of work, wasn't it? It is a strategy that works, but it takes a lot of time. I'm wondering if it might have been easier to just add up all the boxes of each kind first? Did you give any thought to that? If you had 24 shipping boxes would you know how many cubes that is?

Tanisha: Well, I know that there are 1,000 cubes in each box, so maybe... 24,000?

Author's notes

Diana asks for permission to confer, and then starts the conferral by listening and getting clarification. The pair has used a splitting/expanded notation strategy. First, they decomposed each number into expanded notation, and then they used partial sums to determine the total. Diana points out that while their strategy works, it is taking a great deal of work and time. She does not tell them what to do, but instead offers an invitation

Diana: Wow! You did that quickly! Do you think she is right, Jared?	*to consider whether the boxes could be added first. By doing so, she encourages them to consider ahead what the digits in each column refer to.*
Jared: *(pondering)* Oh yeah! Tanisha, we could just add up the boxes. That's a lot easier... and then we just know how many cubes that is!	
Diana: Say more about that.	*Diana asks for more clarification. Encouraging Jared to say more supports him to reflect and deepen his thinking.*
Jared: If there are 24 shipping boxes, there are 24,000 cubes. And if there are 4 pallets, there are 400 cubes. We could just add the boxes! That's a lot easier!	
Diana: Wow! What a great insight. This will be a faster approach, won't it? This will be worth sharing in the congress later. Mathematicians do like efficiency, don't they?	*Diana celebrates what they have done and explicitly asks them to convince the community of this discovery.*

Facilitating the Math Congress

No gallery walk is needed today as most work will probably have been done directly on Appendix B. Choose a few work samples that you can use for the congress, however, ensuring that discussion occurs on the efficiency of repacking as one works from right to left. For example, look for a work sample where the students show an understanding of the value of the boxes and they have simply added the number of each type of box. If a pair has worked randomly (for example: starting with pallets, going to longs, and then adding shipping boxes), you might have them start the congress, using their work sample for a discussion on why the boxes can just be added and totals can be decomposed with the numbers placed in appropriate columns. This brings the big idea that *place determines value* up for discussion. Next have a group that moved right to left, regrouping systematically as they added. Invite discussion on how efficient this strategy is. If numbers are decomposed and parts are placed in the right columns (thinking of the value as a box, or power of ten), the amounts are still equivalent, and the adding is easier. Look at students' work with an eye to the big ideas and strategies on the landscape and you will see the potential for many rich discussions.

Reflections on the Day

Today provided students with a chance to explore regrouping. Carrying was introduced and used throughout the day, first in the minilesson and then later in the investigation. By using the context of boxes and packaging, students naturally come to understand how the powers of ten that they explored during the first few days of this unit, can now be used for column addition. On Days Six through Ten, as students play more rounds of the game and engage in buying and selling, they will have further opportunities to practice this addition strategy and will also work with the subtraction algorithm.

DAY SIX

THE GAME BEGINS

Materials Needed

Game Rules
(Appendix F, one per
student and for
projection)

Driver Sales Ledger
(Appendix G, one per
student and for
projection)

Sales Cards
(Appendix H, one full
deck per company)

End of Day Summary
(Appendix I, one per
company)

Gameboard
(Appendix J, one per
company)

Truck Game Pieces
(tokens or chips, one
per student)

Calculators, one per
company

Today students play round one of the game they prepared for on Day Five. The game continues throughout the week with one round played each day. As employees of the companies they formed, students become truck drivers who make deliveries. Each driver picks up 10 shipping boxes from the warehouse to start and records transactions required by the game cards. The standard addition and subtraction algorithms emerge as players unpack and pack boxes to record transactions, calculate what is left in their trucks, and total the amounts of cubes sold. Players also round to the nearest 1,000 as they move along the gameboard.

Day Six Outline

Developing the Context
❖ Convene students in the meeting area to introduce the game, explain the rules of play, and demonstrate how transactions are recorded.
❖ Explain how to round to the nearest 1,000 and show how players track their progress using rounding.
❖ Once everyone is clear on the directions, send them off in company groups to play.

Supporting the Investigation
❖ As students play, move around and support them as needed. Note the strategies they use to add, subtract, and record their transactions.
❖ Use the context to generate the algorithms by asking what boxes need to be opened to make the delivery and what boxes need to be refilled to organize the materials in the truck.

Math Journals
❖ At the end of a round of play, invite students to reflect in their journals about strategies they used to add, subtract, and record their transactions.

Developing the Context

Gather students in the meeting area to introduce the game. Remind students that when they formed companies on Day Five and took inventory of their warehouses, each company determined that they had 100,000 cubes in their warehouses. Explain that today the companies will meet again, but today each player will be a driver who makes sales and deliveries for their company. Drivers begin the game with 10,000 puzzle cubes (10 shipping boxes) from the company warehouse in their trucks.

Pass out copies of the directions (Appendix F) to each student and project a copy for all to see. [Note: Digital versions of the appendices can be found on the CFLM online support system, P2S2: a personalized professional support system™, found at www.NewPerspectivesOnline.net.] Go through the directions with the class and then pass out one copy of the Driver Sales Ledger (Appendix G) to each student and project a sample copy for the community to see. Explain that each company will have a deck of sales cards. The decks should each be shuffled, and 18 cards should be counted out and turned face down. On Days Six through Nine, a round of the game will be played each day using a new set of 18 randomly-drawn cards. In each round, players will take turns drawing a card and reading it aloud, then work simultaneously to record the transaction on their individual Driver Sales Ledgers. Each time, as boxes are unpacked to make deliveries, the unpacking should also be recorded in the unpacking area on the sheet along with the subtraction showing what remains in the truck. Trucks should be kept organized with materials in full boxes (packed maximally).

> ## Behind the Numbers
>
> Having students start with 10,000 cubes each day guarantees that regrouping (borrowing) will be needed as shipping boxes will need to be unpacked to make deliveries of the sales. Also, at the end of each day, regrouping (this time carrying) will be required as students repack to total the sales made and check that the total of cubes remaining in the truck and cubes sold add up to 10,000. Each truck and company warehouse should also be organized at the end of each day with everything maximally packed into full boxes. Cubes remaining in the warehouse and cubes sold should always add up to 100,000, although money will not add up in the same way because of the expenses and outside gains and losses.

Once all players have read their first cards, they work to determine the number of cubes they each have left in their trucks, recording the transaction on their sales ledgers. They check each other's work to make sure they agree no mistakes in accounting have been made and then each player checks the transaction with a calculator. If the calculator shows a mistake has been made, players work together to find it and correct errors as needed. Once agreement is reached, players each round the number of cubes left in their trucks to the nearest thousand and place their truck piece at that point on the game board.

Play continues with each player taking a second card. Transactions are again recorded, amounts left in the truck are rounded to the nearest thousand, and players move along the game board accordingly. Play continues until all 18 cards are used (some students may have one more turn than others).

Supporting the Investigation

As you walk around supporting and conferring with students, note the strategies they are using for the subtraction. Appendix G, the sales ledger, is designed in the form of a place value chart on purpose to support students to make use of place value and to suggest packing and unpacking boxes (regrouping) as needed to make sales. Don't try to explain the algorithms first or direct students to do the steps of the algorithm directly by telling them to start with the ones. Just stay grounded in the context as you confer, asking students what boxes they will need to open to make the delivery. Support them to record in the regrouping/repacking area on their ledgers and question them about equivalence. Ensure that they realize the amount they have after unpacking whatever was needed to make the transaction is equivalent to the amount they had earlier—the cubes have just been reorganized to allow for the delivery. On this first day of the game, be prepared to see quite a bit of inefficient regrouping as described in the Overview. Remember that the landscape describes development. Students will regroup without meaning if they do not think about what is in the box they are opening. Others may regroup meaningfully but inefficiently. These attempts are wonderful moments to support development because they allow students to grapple with many of the ideas on the landscape that underlie performing the algorithms flexibly and efficiently. For example, many students will struggle trying to remember the value (power of ten) of each box. Others may not even see the need to unpack and make the common errors we often see when trying to subtract from zero; they may just copy the digit in the minuend and assume it is the difference. Still others may regroup everything (opening every box) even when it is not needed. Stay in the context and simply ask these students if all the boxes need to be opened. Explain that good drivers do not drive messy trucks as puzzle cubes can be lost and messy trucks require time to repack. Explain that it's not only mathematicians who like efficiency; so do company owners who often say "time is money!"

Here are some strategies you can anticipate:

❖ Regrouping without meaning: crossing numbers out to show a box has been opened but not thinking about the value of the box, only moving digits. Figure 14 shows how a pallet has been opened (going from 4 to 3), but the 3 was first placed in front of the 0 in the tens place, producing 30. Realizing this was wrong, the student wrote "13" (still using the 3 but adding 10) and then made this 12 when she unpacked to get 12 loose units. As you confer with students like these, ask them what box they are opening and what they have taken out. Focus on what is in the box they opened. Help them see that if they had 0 long boxes and they opened a pallet that had 10 long boxes in it, they now have 10 long boxes. Use the base-ten blocks to model the action if needed and support the student to record the results.

Unpacking/Repacking Area	Shipping boxes	Pallets	~~12 to 9~~ Long Boxes	Loose Units
Beginning Totals →	8	~~4~~ 3	~~30~~ ~~13~~	12
Transaction: Hats			6	5
What's left on the truck	8	3	~~3~~ 4	7

Figure 14: Regrouping without meaning for 8,402 – 65.

❖ Inefficient regrouping: starting with the largest boxes first and opening every box even when it is not necessary. Students may subtract the shipping boxes first, then the pallets, longs, and loose units, unpacking and regrouping to add 10 to the next smaller box but often needing to regroup again at the end of the problem (see Figure 15a). Sometimes this inefficiency can result in so much repacking that confusion results even when students do know the value of the boxes (see Figure 15b). As you confer, stay in the context and invite consideration on whether all the different boxes need unpacking. Point out examples where the order could be taken to the customer without unpacking. Once students see that not all boxes need to be opened you might suggest that starting with the loose units and unpacking boxes only when it is needed might be more efficient.

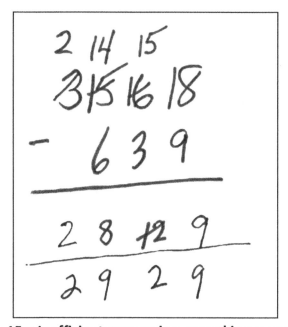

Figure 15a: Inefficient regrouping, repacking everything.

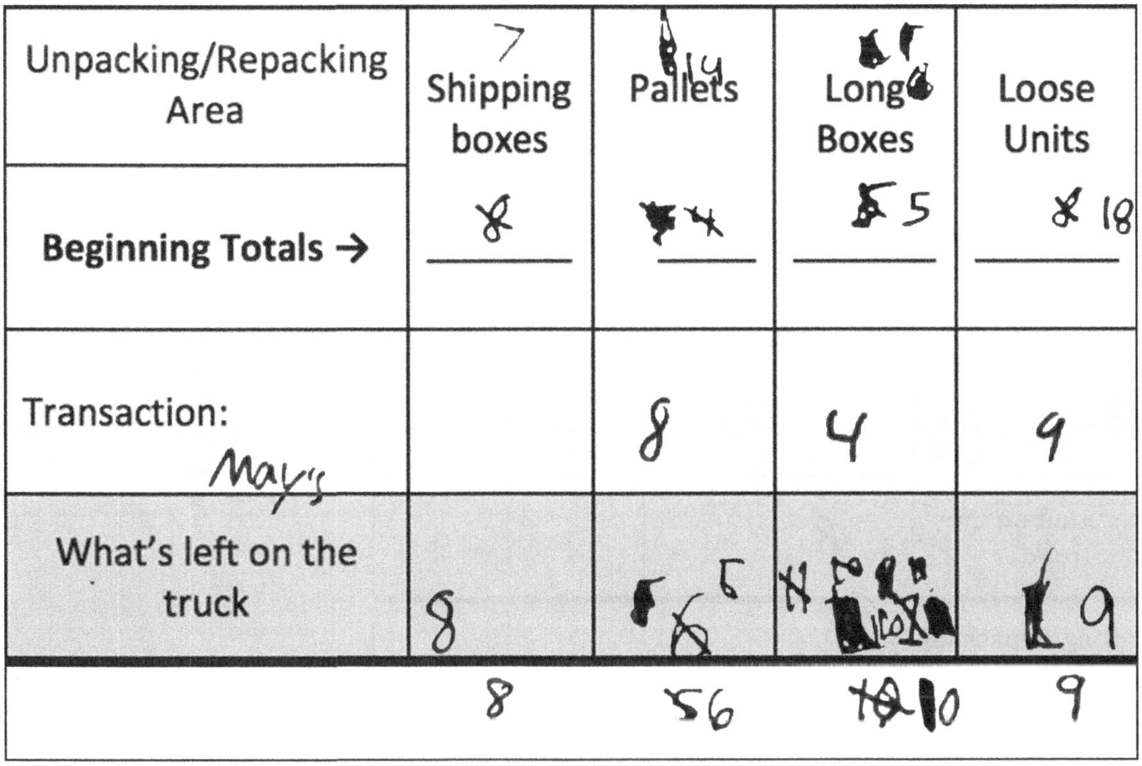

Unpacking/Repacking Area	Shipping boxes	Pallets	Long Boxes	Loose Units
Beginning Totals →	7 / 8	14 / 4	5	18 / 8
Transaction: May's		8	4	9
What's left on the truck	8	6 / 5	(regrouped)	9
	8	56	10	9

Figure 15b: Repacking everything so many times that confusion results.

❖ Using a separate piece of paper or math journal to use known strategies for subtraction, solving the problem without considering the unpacking and regrouping at all. These students will simply use the ledger as a place to fill in answers. As you confer, support the preservation of good number sense and efficiency while encouraging the student to consider the unpacking and regrouping that is part of the context. Remind them of the truck and the fact that the driver only has shipping boxes at the start and that all transactions need to be recorded and checked.

❖ Using the standard algorithm flexibly and efficiently: starting with the loose cubes and unpacking a long box if necessary, then a pallet, then a shipping box, and continuing in this manner of regrouping to ensure there is always an adequate amount of the appropriate unit from which to subtract (see Figure 16a). The beauty of this strategy is that the regrouping is done with fewer steps—often just once per place, and only if needed. And of course, this is what underlies the use of the algorithm and why, before the advent of calculators, the algorithms were the primary ways accounting was done. They required less time and paper. There are other ways to regroup efficiently, so be alert and support them as well. For example, see Figure 16b where the regrouping, when needed, is done almost mentally within the difference at the bottom, rather than at the top. The regrouping here is solidly understood and used flexibly.

Starting total of merchandise: **10000** cubes

Unpacking/Repacking Area	Shipping Boxes	Pallets	Long Boxes	Loose Units	Use this space to add up the number of cubes you sold.
Beginning Totals →	10 (9)	10 (9)	10 (9)	10	
Transaction: Amarica	1	7	7	6	
What's left on the truck	8	2	2	4	
Unpacking/Repacking Area	Shipping Boxes (7)	Pallets	Long Boxes	Loose Units	
Beginning Totals →	8	12 11	12 11	14	
Transaction: monica		8	4	8	
What's left on the truck	7	3	7	6	
Unpacking/Repacking Area	Shipping Boxes (6)	Pallets	Long Boxes	Loose Units	
Beginning Totals →	7	13	7	6	
Transaction: nax	1	9	7	0	
What's left on the truck	5	4	0	6	

Handwritten work (right column):

```
1776
 848
1970
2 4414
4 4 44
  5 9

4594
```

```
2660
  82
1227
3869
  16
```

```
8552
```

```
3969        3969
4596        4596
14443       14443
8555        8555
```

Figure 16a: Using the standard algorithm flexibly and efficiently.

Unpacking/Repacking Area	Shipping Boxes	Pallets	Long Boxes	Loose Units
Beginning Totals →	5	5	7	0
Transaction:		4	4	2
What's left on the truck	5	1	~~3~~ ~~2~~ ~~1~~	~~0~~ 8

Figure 16b: Using the standard algorithm flexibly and efficiently by regrouping within the difference.

As students are playing, move around the room and observe their strategies for both adding and subtracting. Be sure to check in with the students you noted during the minilesson on Day Five who may need support to play the game. Ask them to explain their work in terms of the unpacking and regrouping they are doing, and challenge them to imagine the delivery truck and whether what they are doing would make sense given the context. You may need to support their understanding of the role of place in the number's value; for example, 5 pallets is 500 loose units, which is 10 times more than the quantity in 5 long boxes. Remember that your goal is to support students' understanding and development of the standard algorithm, but not to encourage them to override efficient strategies and number sense. If a student makes a sale of 999 cubes, encourage them to reason about the number relationships, removing 1,000 (opening a shipping box) and adding 1 back in rather than unpacking 9 pallets, 9 longs, and 9 units. As you are observing and checking in, this is also a good opportunity for you to document students' learning by taking a picture of their work. The New Perspectives on Assessment web-based app (www.NewPerspectivesOnAssessment.com) is an ideal way to do this. You can even take a quick 30-second video!

Some companies may not have gotten through all 18 transactions to complete a day of driving in this session, but some will be ready to check their totals before the end of the class period. You may decide to call a couple of companies to the rug to demonstrate what happens at the end of a day of driving and let the others continue playing. Alternately, you can bring everyone together and show Appendix I on the document camera or projector and demonstrate how each driver will total the number of cubes sold and the number of cubes left on the truck (which should equal 10,000). Each company will then calculate their totals and earnings for the day. Remind students to use calculators to check their work when completing Appendix I.

Diana (the teacher): How's the game going? May I sit and confer with you?

Alana: Sure. *(She reads a card.)* It says I sold 2,489 cubes. I have 9,918 in my truck, so that's 9 shipping boxes, and I'll take away 2, that's 7. I have 9 pallets, take away 4, that's 5. Hmmm. I only have 1 long box, and I need 8, so I'll cross out the 9 [pallets] and make it 8. Now I have 11 long boxes, take away 8, that's 3. But now I have to change my pallets to 4 *(going back to the pallets column and changing the 5 to 4).* Now I have 8 units, I need 9, so I'll change my long boxes to 10, and now I have to change my answer to 2, and now I have 18 units, take away 9, that's 9.

Diana: Whew! That was a lot of steps. So what's your answer?

Alana: 7, 5—no I mean 4, 2, 9. I think it's 7,429.

Diana: You seem like you're not sure, and mathematicians like to prove their work. How can you be sure?

Alana: Well, it's either 7,529 or 7,429. I'll just do it again to see if I get the same answer. It's just that I crossed the numbers out a couple of times so, hmmm…

Diana: I noticed that you started with the shipping boxes, then went from left to right, then back. That's a lot of unpacking and repacking! What if you started with the units?

Alana: I'll try it. *(She repeats the work, beginning with the loose units and moving from right to left.)* I'll unpack a long box, make this 18, then unpack a pallet, make this into 10 long boxes and subtract. It's 7,429. That was only 4 steps and I'm done!

Diana: Wow! That made it a lot easier. Do you think you could share this in the congress later? It could be helpful to lots of other kids, too.

Author's notes

Diana asks for permission to confer, and then starts the conferral by listening and getting clarification. She notes that Alana is regrouping with meaning but doing so inefficiently.

Note how Diana focuses on efficiency and proof. This is a nice mentoring move as she is modeling what mathematicians do.

Math Journals

Remember to allot some time at the end of the work period for students to reflect in their math journals. In writing about their strategies and discoveries, students will begin to make judgments about which strategies are most effective and efficient. In articulating their ideas, students may also need to refer back to the work they did with powers of ten at the beginning of the unit. Don't underestimate the importance of this time to evaluate and synthesize ideas!

Reflections on the Day

As you observed and supported the students during the game, you were able to see the strategies they were using for addition and subtraction. Day Seven begins with a minilesson on subtraction using quick images, so students will have opportunities to examine more efficient approaches and try them out.

DAY SEVEN

ROUND TWO

Today begins with a quick image minilesson on subtraction, crafted to further support students with regrouping as they prepare to repack more boxes in the game. Students then play round two of the game. The standard addition and subtraction algorithms will continue to emerge as players unpack and pack boxes to record transactions, calculate what is left in their trucks, and total the amounts of cubes sold. Players also continue to round to the nearest 1,000 as they move along the gameboard.

Day Seven Outline

Minilesson: What's left in the truck?
❖ Work on a string of quick images designed to encourage the use of place value and regrouping when subtracting.

Supporting the Investigation
❖ As students play, move around and support them as needed. Note the strategies they use to add, subtract, and record their transactions.
❖ Use the context to generate the algorithms by asking what boxes need to be opened to make each delivery and what boxes need to be refilled to organize the materials in the truck.

Math Journals
❖ At the end of a round of play, invite students to reflect in their journals about strategies they used.

Materials Needed

Quick Image Cards
(three copies of two cards from Appendix E as noted in the text)

Driver Sales Ledger
(Appendix G, one per student and for projection)

Sales Cards
(Appendix H, one full deck per company)

End of Day Summary
(Appendix I, one per company)

Gameboard
(Appendix J, one per company)

Truck Game Pieces
(tokens or chips, one per student)

Calculators, one per company

Minilesson: What's left in the truck?

Today's minilesson uses two of the quick image cards from Appendix E that you used on Day Five. However, now the cards are used differently to foster more efficient regrouping when subtracting—a different goal than the goal of Day Five. Use the card from Appendix E, designated in the string below as the minuend, and write the subtrahend *in numerals* directly underneath it, carefully lining up amounts in appropriate place value columns. Make the image visible for a few seconds and then remove it. Ask, "What boxes do you need to open, and what's left in the truck?" When students have had enough think time and the discussion starts, make the image visible again.

The String

$321 - 9$

$321 - 39$

$321 - 139$

$1,042 - 3$

$1,042 - 403$

$1,042 - 1,003$

Behind the Numbers

The numbers have been chosen carefully to support students to regroup minimally and to think about precisely where the regrouping needs to occur. The first problem makes use of a single digit minuend, as a helper to the next two problems. Only one box needs to be opened—one of the longs (a ten). Many students may say they would just remove a long box and add a unit back in. This is a terrific mental math strategy for getting the answer and you can celebrate that they used this strategy to subtract. However, the first question asks what boxes need to be opened to make the delivery. Stay in the context and remind students of the question: "What would the driver need to open to make the delivery?" A long box needs to be unpacked (making 11 loose puzzle cubes and removing 9 for the delivery). Nothing else needs to be opened. As you record this during the discussion, write the minuend and subtrahend in numerals, stacked in columns, and represent the regrouping with the traditional notation for the standard algorithm by crossing out the 2 and writing a 1 above it and making the 1 in the units column into an 11. With the next problem most students will likely use the information from the first problem and say that now a pallet needs to be opened as well. Add this information to the earlier representation, crossing out the 3, making it a 2, and making the 1 in the tens column into an 11. Ensure that students understand that this notation is only showing the boxes being opened and that the repacking does not affect the amount of cubes in the truck until a delivery is made and cubes are removed. If students do not make use of the first problem then record exactly what they do, showing the regrouping.

Developing the Context

Gather students in the meeting area and have a brief discussion to remind them of the rules of the game. Invite discussion on challenges they may have encountered in the first round and questions they may have. Establish that all records of accounting from each day are kept in their company binders, and on the last day of play everything will be totaled. But, at the start of each day drivers always begin with an empty truck and pick up 10 new, unopened shipping boxes as they start the day's deliveries.

Pass out copies of all the appendices needed for play and send students off in company groups for another round, using a new set of 18 cards from a shuffled deck of sales cards. Remind students that all players should read their first cards aloud and then simultaneously work to determine the number of cubes they each have left in their truck, recording the transaction on their sales ledgers, checking each other's work to make sure they agree no mistakes in accounting have been made, and then checking all transactions with the company's calculator. If the calculator shows a mistake has been made, players should work together to find it and correct errors as needed. Once agreement is reached, players each round the number of cubes left in their trucks to the nearest thousand and place their truck piece at that point on the game board. As in round one, play continues with each player taking a second card. Transactions are again recorded, amounts left in the truck are rounded to the nearest thousand, and players move along the game board accordingly. Play continues until all 18 cards are used.

Supporting the Investigation

As you walk around supporting and conferring with students, note the strategies they are using for the subtraction, just as you did during round one. Remember that Appendix G, the sales ledger, is designed in the form of a place value chart on purpose to support students to make use of place value and to suggest packing and unpacking boxes (regrouping) as needed to make sales. Today the minilesson may also be an added support; encourage students to reflect on the problems and discussion from the minilesson as you confer.

Math Journals

Remember to allot some time at the end of the work period for students to reflect in their math journals. Encourage students to write about the ideas that struck them during the minilesson and the new strategies they may have tried out or seen their peers use during the second round today.

Reflections on the Day

As you observed and supported the students during the game, you were able to see the strategies they were using. Their experience on Day Six and the minilesson likely supported students to regroup more efficiently. Examine the work students did during the first round and compare it to the work they did today. Do you see differences? This is a good time to read over the Overview as it will help you understand the development of place value better. The landscape is also a terrific tool for you to use to document the growth (and challenges) you see. You might make copies of the landscape, one for each student's records and document the growth pathways you see with a yellow highlighter. If you prefer, you can do this digitally using our app: www.NewPerspectivesOnAssessment.com.

DAY EIGHT

ROUND THREE

Materials Needed

Two Strategies
(Appendix K)

Driver Sales Ledger
(Appendix G, one per
student and for
projection)

Sales Cards
(Appendix H, one full
deck per company)

End of Day Summary
(Appendix I, one per
company)

Gameboard
(Appendix J, one per
company)

Truck Game Pieces
(tokens or chips, one
per student)

Calculators, one per
company

Pencils

Today begins with a minilesson using a string of related addition problems crafted to support regrouping with addition. Students then play round three of the game. The standard addition and subtraction algorithms will continue to emerge as players unpack and pack boxes to record transactions; by now you will likely be seeing substantial progress. Players also continue to round to the nearest 1,000 as they move along the gameboard.

Day Eight Outline

Minilesson: Packing New Boxes

❖ Work on a string of related addition problems designed to encourage the use of place value and regrouping when adding.

Supporting the Investigation

❖ As students play round three, move around and support them as needed. Note the strategies they use to add and how they record their transactions.

❖ Use the context to generate the algorithms by asking what boxes need to be opened to make the delivery and what boxes need to be refilled to organize the materials in the truck.

Journal Writing and Discussion

❖ As groups come to the end of a round of play, invite them to use their journals and write quietly, reflecting on the new strategies they are using in the game as they pack and unpack. Ask them to write about why the strategies work and about how they are connected to the work with powers of ten that they did on the first two days of the unit. This writing will prepare students for the subsequent discussion.

❖ Bring everyone to the meeting area to reflect on two different regrouping strategies and invite discussion on why they both work.

Minilesson: Packing New Boxes

Today's minilesson is a string of related addition problems. Write each problem in stacked fashion as shown below, one at a time, inviting discussion on the following questions: "What new boxes can be packed, and how many puzzle cubes are there in total?" If your students still need base-ten support, you can use the image from Appendix E to show the first addend for the first four problems and encourage students to mentally image adding the second addend. Represent their strategies by placing the quantity of newly filled boxes in the appropriate column (showing carrying). In the first three problems only one new box can be made—a long. In the fourth problem a shipping box can also be made. The last problem is a challenge. After writing all four addends, provide pair talk for reflection and discussion. Here, 2 long boxes can be filled after adding up the loose units. Adding the longs produces a new pallet, and once again a new shipping box can also be filled.

The String (in order from left to right):

321	321	321	321	343
+ 9	+ 39	+ 139	+ 839	847
				138
				+ 2

Supporting the Investigation

Gather students in the meeting area and have a brief discussion to remind them of the rules of the game, if needed, and to see if there are any questions. Remind them that at the start of each day drivers always pick up 10 new, unopened shipping boxes as they start the day's deliveries. Pass out copies of all appendices needed for play and send students off in company groups for another round, using a new set of 18 cards from a shuffled deck of sales cards. Remind them that all players should read their cards aloud and then work simultaneously to determine the number of cubes they each have left in their truck, recording the transaction on their sales ledgers. They should then, as before, check each other's work to make sure they agree no mistakes in accounting have been made. All transactions should then be checked with the company's calculator. If the calculator shows a mistake has been made, players should work together to find it and correct errors as needed. Once agreement is reached, players each round the number of cubes left in their trucks to the nearest thousand and place their truck piece at that point on the game board. Play continues until all 18 cards are used. As you walk around supporting and conferring with students, note the strategies they are now using for both addition and subtraction, looking for growth. If you still see students challenged to compute effectively, sit and confer to determine what is at the root of their struggles. This is now the third day playing the game and most students will likely be showing some nice growth along the landscape. As you confer, remind students who are still challenged of discussions and examples from the minilessons.

Journal Writing and Discussion

Company groups will likely finish the round at different times. As groups finish, move them into quiet journal writing, inviting them to reflect on the new strategies they are using for addition and subtraction in the game (and in the minilessons). Ask them to write about why these regrouping strategies work and about how they are connected to the work with powers of ten that they did on the first two days of the unit. This writing will prepare students for a subsequent discussion.

Once every company finishes the round, bring everyone to the meeting area to reflect on two different regrouping strategies and why they both work. Start by displaying the two strategies shown on Appendix K. Explain that over the years you have seen students use many versions of regrouping strategies once they become very familiar with how the boxes are related. Ask students to look at the work and see if they can figure out what the two students have done, if both strategies work, and if so, why. Provide pair talk and move around and listen in to some of the discussions to learn how your students are talking about the questions; this will help you facilitate the discussion when you convene the whole group.

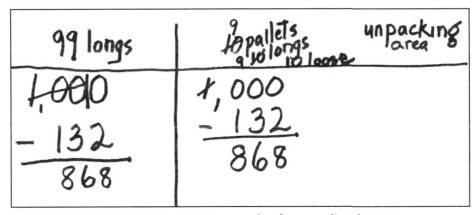

Figure 17: Two Samples (Appendix K)

Teacher Note:

The student in the first sample looked at the numbers first and immediately saw the need to regroup to get a ten into the units column. Rather than proceeding column by column, as in the standard algorithm shown in sample two, the shipping box is seen as having 100 longs and so 1 ten is placed in the units column immediately, leaving 99 remaining, effectively doing the regrouping needed in one move rather than tediously working from column to column. This is a good example of flexibly using the algorithm, regrouping efficiently as needed. To understand why It works, students must revisit the ideas they discussed earlier in the unit as they constructed the big idea that place matters. The number can be shifted to the right or left depending on the question asked. If one wants to know how many tens are in 1,000, one can simply shift focus over to the left one place, effectively dividing by ten. There are 100 tens in 1,000. This strategy will likely be more challenging to understand than the second sample. The purpose of the discussion is not to push one strategy to be used over another, however. Its sole purpose is to bring forth a discussion on why both work. Equivalence through regrouping gets to the heart of both strategies.

Reflections on the Day

Today you likely witnessed a powerful discussion on several big ideas and strategies on the landscape: that place matters, regrouping and equivalence, and flexible and efficient ways to regroup to subtract and add using the standard algorithm. If you would like to see a video of discussion on the two samples shown in Appendix K, go to P2S2: a personalized professional support system™. If your school does not have the platform and you want information about it, go to www.NewPerspectivesOnline.net.

As you observed and supported the students during the minilesson and as you conferred during the game, you were likely able to glean more about each student's thinking and where he or she is on the landscape. If you didn't yesterday, take time reading over the Overview (or view Cathy talking about that, too, on the platform) as it will help you understand the development of place value better. The landscape is also a terrific tool for you to use to document the growth (and challenges) you see. You can do this by hand with paper copies of the landscape and a yellow highlighter, or if you prefer you can do this digitally using our app: www.NewPerspectivesOnAssessment.com.

DAY NINE

ROUNDING TO THE NEAREST HUNDRED

Materials Needed

Driver Sales Ledgers, Sales Cards, End of Day Summaries, Gameboards, Truck Game Pieces, and **Calculators** as on previous days

Delivery Routes (Appendix L, one copy for display)

Address Cards (Appendix M, one deck)

Life Cards (Appendix N, one deck)

Today begins with a minilesson on rounding to the nearest hundred. Students work to place flags marking addresses (Appendix M) along a delivery route where landmark hundreds are shown (Appendix L). A last round of the game is then played and final accounting of transactions over the course of the four rounds is done. Companies then each randomly choose a card from a shuffled deck of "Life Cards" (Appendix N) and do final accounting to determine the overall winner of the game.

Day Nine Outline

Minilesson: Delivery Routes

❖ Display Appendix L showing two delivery routes. Pass out address cards from Appendix M, one to each pair, asking pairs to approximate where each address is on the route.

❖ Ask pairs, one at a time, to share where they think the address is located and to justify their thinking to the group. Invite discussion until agreement is reached, marking the location with a flag.

❖ Once all the flags are placed, explain that drop-offs will occur only at the nearest hundred mark and customers will need to decide which location is the closest.

Supporting the Investigation

❖ As students play round four, move around and support them as needed. When the round is over, companies choose a life card (Appendix N) and do final accounting to determine which company has won the game.

Minilesson: Delivery Routes

Today's minilesson is designed to foster students' abilities to round numbers in the thousands to the nearest 100. Display the map of the two delivery routes shown on Appendix L, using a smart board or document camera. [If you do not have this technology available you can just draw two routes (open number lines) on a large white board, marking the starting and end points of each.] Explain that you will pass out a card to each pair of students showing a street address that a driver needs to find. The map shows two different routes. They will need to determine which route they should take and approximately where on the route the address is. Shuffle the deck of cards from Appendix M and pass out one card to each pair of students. Provide pairs with time to talk and justify their determinations and then invite pairs to go to the display one at a time, point out where they think the address is on the map, and justify their decision to the group. Invite whole class discussion until consensus is reached. Mark all agreed upon points with flags and write the numbers on the flags. Once all flags are placed, explain that delivery drop-offs will occur only at the marked hundreds. Customers will need to round to the nearest hundred to determine where they should go for pick-up. Provide pair talk and then invite discussion on each marked point. Students will likely come up with a rule for numbers over the midpoint (5 tens). Let them discuss this a bit to ensure everyone understands why this discussion matters—how consistency is important, or customers will go to the wrong location. Then explain that mathematicians have had a similar debate and decided for consistency purposes to always round up when the digit in the column to the right is 5 or above, and to round down when the value is 4 or below.

> **Teacher Note:**
>
> The design of the minilesson provides students with a context to round numbers in the thousands to the nearest hundred. At first students estimate and justify their placements of the numbers on the delivery routes. Support them to think about the magnitude of the address numbers in relation to any nearby landmark numbers. For example, if a pair placing #3,435 says, "We know it is between #3,000 and #4,000," ask which thousand it is closer to and how they know. If they then say, "The number is between #3,400 and #3,500," ask which hundred it is closer to and how they know. At this point in the minilesson, it is only magnitude and nearness to landmarks that you want to focus on. Support them to come up with good estimates of the exact location for each address. After all flags are placed, the conversation will shift to rounding to the nearest drop-off location. The early part of the conversation is designed to support the underlying understanding of number magnitude. Rounding meaningfully is not possible if the magnitude of numbers in relation to landmarks is not understood. Many textbooks teach rounding as a rote skill or procedure: look to the digit in the column to the right of the value you are rounding to and if it is 5 or over round up. If it is under 5, round down. When taught this way, students often have no understanding of number relations. They memorize the rule, and later misapply or forget it.

Supporting the Investigation

Gather students in the meeting area and have a brief discussion to remind them of the rules of the game, if needed, and to see if there are any questions. Remind them that at the start of each day drivers always pick up 10 new unopened shipping boxes as they start the day's deliveries. Pass out copies of all appendices needed for play and send students off in company groups for the last round, using a new set of 18 cards from a shuffled deck of sales cards. Remind them that all players should read their cards aloud and then work simultaneously to determine the number of cubes they each have left in their truck, recording the transaction on their sales ledgers. They should then, as before, check each other's work to make sure they agree no mistakes in accounting have been made. All transactions should then be checked with the company's calculator. If the calculator shows a mistake has been made, players should work together to find it and correct errors as needed. Once agreement is reached, players each round the number of cubes left in their trucks to the nearest thousand and place their truck piece at that point on the game board. Play continues until all 18 cards are used. As you walk around supporting and conferring with students, note the strategies they are now using for both addition and subtraction, looking for growth. If you still see students challenged to compute efficiently, sit and confer to determine what is at the root of their struggles. This is now the last day playing the game and most students should be showing growth along the landscape towards fluency and flexibility with the algorithms for addition and subtraction. If you have students still challenged by the algorithms, bring them together for more focused work with you using minilessons like the ones you did earlier in the week. Once most students are done with the round, ask them to get their company books ready for an audit. They should check all calculations with a calculator and total the amounts of cubes sold during the week and the gross profit made. If they find any errors in their calculations, they should redo them and fix errors so that they are sure the figure of gross income from sales of all four rounds is correct.

Shuffle the deck of Life Cards (Appendix N) and then turn them over so that they are face down. Have a representative from each company come up and choose a card. The result of the card should be added (or subtracted as the case may be) to the gross profit to determine gross income. Draw an open number line and as companies report their gross income ask students in the company to determine approximately where the number should go on the line. Once all numbers are on the line ask students to reflect on the differences and the relations, reminding them that all sales were determined by "luck of the draw." Are the distances between the numbers close, far apart, or clustered? Which company was the luckiest? Is there an outlier? After discussion on the differences and relations, write the results in an ordered form using the symbols <, =, and > and announce the company with the highest gross income as the winner.

Reflections on the Day

Today students had opportunities to round and this likely provided you with formative assessment data as you witnessed their justifications regarding magnitude, place value, and nearness to landmarks. As you observed and supported students during the minilesson and as you conferred during the game, you were also likely able to glean more about each student's thinking and where he or she is on the landscape. Keep documenting student progress on the place value landscape and attach evidence. Remember that you can take short video clips with a tablet or cell phone and attach them to student landscapes using the assessment app: www.NewPerspectivesOnAssessment.com.

DAY TEN

BEAT THE CALCULATOR

Materials Needed

An Abacus (or a video about adding and subtracting on an abacus)

A Set of Problems (Appendix O, one copy per pair)

Scissors, one pair per student

Small individual whiteboards and markers (or slates or paper, one per pair of students)

Calculators, one per pair of students

Math Journals

Large sheet of butcher paper cut from a roll for a learning scroll

Markers

Today begins with a brief history of the invention of the handheld calculator and the algorithms it uses. Students will likely be fascinated to think about how calculators work and to learn that several early versions of adding machines made use of the algorithms for addition and subtraction that they have been using during this unit. Today they will have an opportunity to practice the algorithms and to try to outperform a partner who will use the calculator. Reflective writing time is then provided in math journals, and notes from the journals are used to build a community learning scroll for display and further reflection.

Day Ten Outline

Developing the Context

❖ Ask students if they know anything about the invention of the calculator and how calculators add and subtract. Facilitate a brief discussion on their ideas.
❖ Provide the brief history included in the unit or use the website links provided on P2S2: a personalized professional support system™.
❖ Ask students to work in pairs trying to beat the calculator on the problems in the deck of cards provided on Appendix O.

Supporting the Investigation

❖ As students play, move around and take note of their flexibility and fluency for calculating, supporting them as needed.

Math Journals and Building a Learning Scroll

❖ Pass out math journals and ask students to reflect on their learning over the course of the unit.
❖ Bring students back to the meeting area with their journals and ask them to share some of their reflections. Use these reflections to build a community learning scroll.

Developing the Context

Gather students in the meeting area and have a brief discussion on the history of calculating machines. Ask them if they know what strategies calculators use when doing addition and subtraction, or if they know who invented the first machine. After some discussion, share the brief history that follows:

One of the earliest calculating machines known was invented by the French mathematician Blaise Pascal in 1642. It was based on the abacus—a bead frame that had been used in the marketplace in Europe, China, Japan, and Russia for many years. The abacus had columns of beads much like the values of the puzzle cube boxes. The column on the right was for units, on the left of that was a column of beads representing tens, the next column to the left had beads representing hundreds, and so forth. When adding or subtracting, the merchant started on the right with the units first and beads were exchanged just like the exchanging you have been doing with the boxes. Units were regrouped into tens, then hundreds, and so on as needed. Pascal's first machine made use of a somewhat similar strategy based on place value, although he modified it a bit.

According to Wikipedia,

"Pascal began to work on his calculator in 1642, when he was 20 years old. He had been assisting his father, who worked as a tax commissioner, and sought to produce a device which could reduce some of his workload. Pascal received a Royal Privilege in 1649 that granted him exclusive rights to make and sell calculating machines in France. By 1654 he had sold about twenty machines, but the cost and complexity of the Pascaline was a barrier to further sales, and so production ceased in that year.

Pascal's calculator had spoked metal wheel dials, with the digit[s] 0 through 9 displayed around the circumference of each wheel. To input a digit, the user placed a stylus in the corresponding space between the spokes and turned the dial until a metal stop at the bottom was reached (similar to the way the rotary dial of old telephones is used). This displayed the number in the windows at the top of the calculator. Then, one simply redialed the second number to be added, causing the sum of both numbers to appear in the accumulator [and to regroup to the next column as needed]."

Calculators today use more complex programming to increase their speed, but all their algorithms are based in some way on place value and regrouping.

> **Teacher Note:**
>
> There are many websites and videos available on the internet that can easily be found by searching for any of the following: the history of the calculator; how an abacus works; Pascal's adding machine; etc. There are also fun clips to watch on competitions between abacus users. Providing a short video clip or two from sites like these will help the context come alive. Updated links will periodically be provided on P2S2: a personalized professional support system™.

After developing the context, explain that you thought it would be fun for students to try to beat the calculator. Assign partnerships and provide each pair with a calculator, a copy of Appendix O, scissors, a small whiteboard (or paper), and a marker. Ask them to cut out the cards on Appendix O and then to turn them over (face down). A card is then turned over and both players work as quickly as possible to get the answer. One player uses the calculator and punches in the numbers; the other calculates the problem and writes the answer on the whiteboard or paper (the problem is NOT rewritten, only the answer is written). Students then alternate roles, and play continues until all cards are done.

> **Teacher Note:**
>
> Ensure that the player without the calculator does not rewrite the problem. The problems are displayed in column fashion to support the use of place value and it is quite likely that many of the students will be able to do the calculations faster than the calculator because of the time needed to key the numbers into the calculator.

Supporting the Investigation

As you walk around supporting and conferring with students, note whether any students are still challenged with the computation and try to determine why. Are they struggling with place value? Do they understand equivalence, and do they regroup accordingly with meaning? Do they have automaticity with the basic facts? Are they making use of other mental math strategies, mentally doing the algorithms, or even flexibly using an algorithm and modifying it to increase speed? You will likely see a range of development and this is an opportunity to consider how you might continue to support where needed even after the unit ends. Minilessons with small groups can be very helpful. Just because the unit is ending does not mean your work with place value needs to end.

Math Journals and Building a Learning Scroll

As students finish with the set of problems, move them into journal writing by asking them to do an entry about the learning that happened for them over the last ten days. You might find it helpful to provide some focus questions such as the following:

- ❖ "Reflect on your learning over the last ten days. What ideas about place value were new for you?"
- ❖ "What strategies for addition and subtraction have you learned and why do they work?"
- ❖ "What ideas came up in discussions that surprised and interested you?"
- ❖ "What questions do you have about place value that would make for further interesting inquiries?"

After providing sufficient time for reflective writing, ask students to bring their journals and come to the meeting area. Have students sit in a circle and ask a few to share aloud what they have been writing. Support a discussion on several of the ideas and strategies that come up and then begin to build a learning scroll.

A learning scroll is a class display—a sort of "socio-historical" wall documenting the progression of the learning, children's questions, the important ideas constructed over the past two weeks, samples of students' work, and descriptions of their strategies and ideas, including anecdotes of how students' thinking changed over time. It is a document of the progression and emergence of learning over the past two weeks. By making this display available, you allow your students to revisit and reflect on all the wonderful ideas and strategies that emerged as they worked throughout the unit.

In preparation for today's work, use a roll of chart paper and cut out a long length sufficient to cover a bulletin board or a display area in a hallway. Curl and staple the two ends, making a small roll on each end. Staple or tape the scroll to the area to be covered. On the left begin with some of the ideas students came up with in the beginning of the unit. You may need to prod them a bit because they may not remember ten days ago! Remind them of the wonderful insights they had about how each box's value was ten times the one before it and about how this insight helped with multiplication and division by ten. Get them talking about exponents and how adding the exponents of the factors, because they were powers of ten, produced the number of zeros in the product. Remind them of how the shapes repeated in each period and how a truck could not hold 1 million puzzle cubes arranged in a giant cube because it would be too wide to go down the road! Remind them of how scaling and simplifying was a great strategy for division—how it was very helpful for 300/12, for instance. Remind them of the great strategies they developed during the game for addition and subtraction and ask if anyone was able to beat the calculator! Take pictures of student posters and print them on normal size copy paper so you can display some on the scroll as examples of work they did during the ten days.

You may want to provide templates with empty speech bubbles and pictures of your students. Use prompts like "At first I thought…" "Then I realized…" and "A good strategy was…" Attach these student explanations to the learning scroll. Wherever you can, show the developmental emergence of ideas on the landscape in the Overview. Display the scroll in a place where your students, and hopefully also the wider school community, can revisit and reflect on the learning that happened during this unit.

Reflections on the Unit

Algorithms for addition and subtraction—the regrouping procedures—were made popular by the great Arab mathematician Muhammad ibn Musa al-Khwarizmi in the early ninth century. Denis Guedj (1996) describes a bit of the history:

> In the Middle Ages computations were carried out on an abacus, also called a computing
> table, a calculating device resembling a table with columns or ruled horizontal lines; digits

were represented by counters, or apices. From the 12th century on, this type of abacus was progressively replaced by the dust board as a tool of calculations. This development did not come about without a struggle between those who, evoking the ancient Greek mathematician Pythagoras, championed the abacus and those who became masters of algorism, the new Arabic number system. In this competition between the Ancients and Moderns, the former saw themselves as the keepers of the secrets of the art of computation and the defenders of the privileges of the guild of professional calculators... [while] the new [place value] system indisputably marked the democratization of computation. (53–54)

The big advance the algorithms brought about was a shift from calculation on a device to a written representation of the calculation. The power of the procedures was that they produced a record of the actions—results could be checked. Soon, calculating was no longer restricted to the guild of professional calculators.

Arithmetical procedures and the computational writing that documented them became the hallmark of knowledge during the Renaissance and continued to be one of the basics in the elementary school for years. But now we once again have tools that we use to do arithmetical calculations. Our students live in this cyber age. It is no longer necessary that the algorithms be practiced over and over as they are not often helpful or used; most calculations are done with either mental arithmetic or with digital technology. Our students need to know whether the answers provided by the cyber tool are reasonable, though. To do that, a strong sense of number and operation, including a deep understanding of place value, is critical.

As you and your students progressed through this unit the standard algorithms for addition and subtraction were developed. But something much more important was being developed, as well. The algorithms are beautiful, elegant creations. They are generalizable strategies and their beauty derives from the structure of our number system. As students worked with this unit they were studying the structure of the number system, writing arguments, representing that structure with exponents, and doing mathematics. The depth of their understanding of powers of ten and the properties of operations that developed as a result will provide a strong foundation for the algebra on their learning horizons. But more than that, students were seeing mathematics as a beautiful creation. And, as the mathematician Danica McKellar once said, "One of the most amazing things about mathematics is that the people who do math aren't usually interested in application, because mathematics itself is truly a beautiful art form. It's about structures and patterns; that's what we love, and that's what we get off on."

How many puzzle cubes does each box hold?

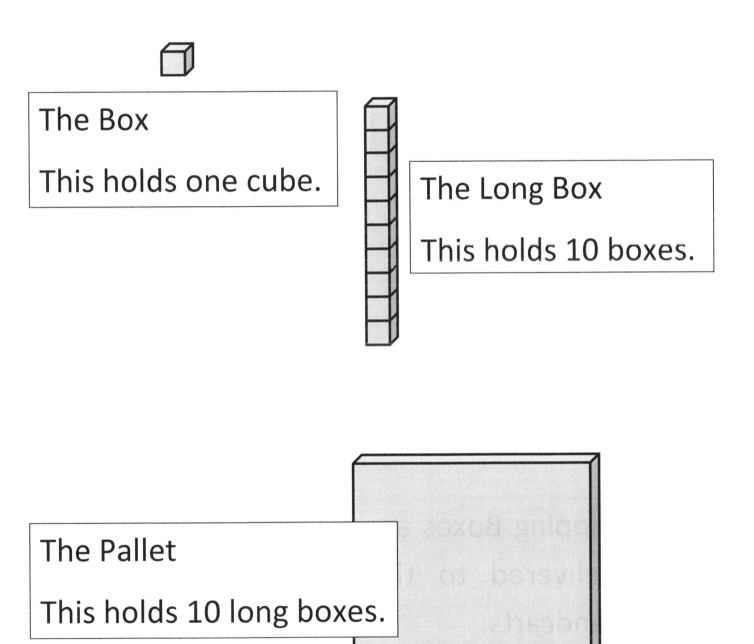

The Box

This holds one cube.

The Long Box

This holds 10 boxes.

The Pallet

This holds 10 long boxes.

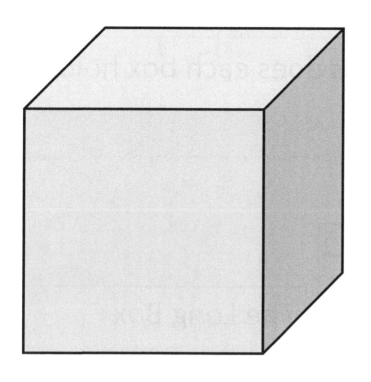

The Shipping Box

This holds 10 pallets.

The Shipping Boxes are rolled and delivered to the truck with handcarts.

The factory worker first makes a row of 10 shipping boxes when the truck is being loaded. It looks sort of like a giant long box!

Then 9 more rows go in and now it looks like a giant pallet! The giant pallet has 100 shipping boxes in it!

When the truck is full it has 10 giant pallets and it looks like a massive cube!! A real truckload! How many puzzle cubes does the truck hold? It has just one massive cube.

Challenge: Puzzle cubes are usually 3x3x3". How big would the truck need to be to hold all those cubes? Could it still go down the road?

Appendix B – Inventory Recording Sheet

Employee Name _____   Date _____

Inventory Total

SECTION	SHIPPING BOXES	PALLETS	LONGS	UNITS
One				
Two				
Three				
Total				

Total Dollar Value of Inventory: $_____

Appendix C – Total Company Inventory Sheet

Company Name _____   Date _____

Company Inventory Total

EMPLOYEE	SHIPPING BOXES	PALLETS	LONGS	UNITS
Initials: _____				
Initials: _____				
Initials: _____				
Initials: _____				
Initials: _____				
Final Total				

Total Dollar Value of Inventory: $_____

Appendix D – Inventory for a company with 4 employees

Printing instructions: Cut out each row and place one row in each envelope. Ensure that all four rows go to four students working together in the same company.

1,321	18,688	3,463
2,342	15,263	6,438
4,757	12,684	10,639
4,652	13,666	6,087

Printing instructions: Cut out each row and place one row in each envelope. Ensure that all five rows go to five students working together in the same company.

4,398	15,235	2,478
4,346	9,367	6,049
7,407	12,784	8,277
2,318	309	10,386
3,020	11,869	1,757

Appendix D – Inventory for a company with 3 employees

Printing instructions: Cut out each row and place one row in each envelope. Ensure that all three rows go to three students working together in the same company.

14,708	15,235	8,078
4,346	9,361	6,049
9,020	21,866	11,337

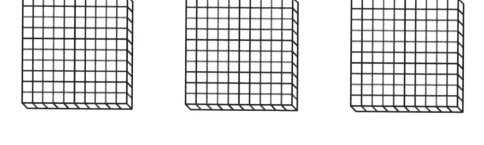

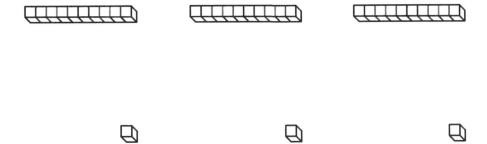

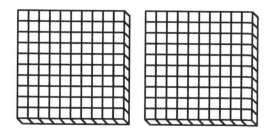

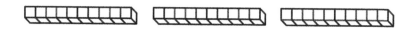

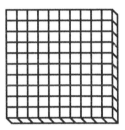

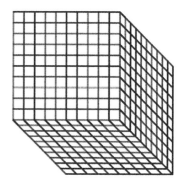

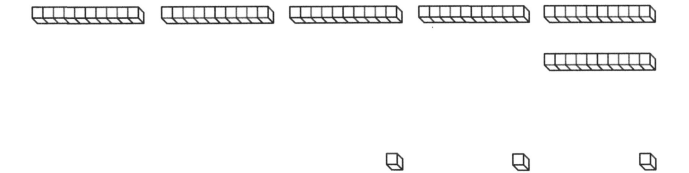

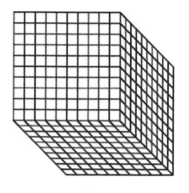

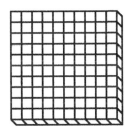

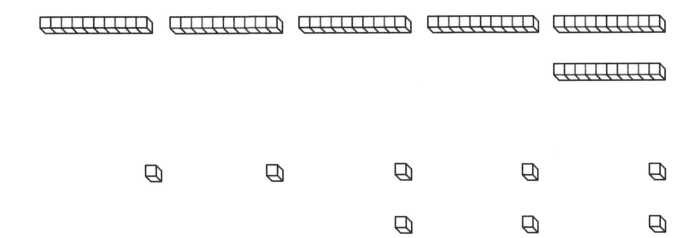

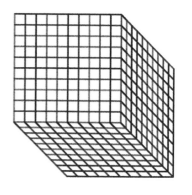

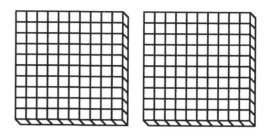

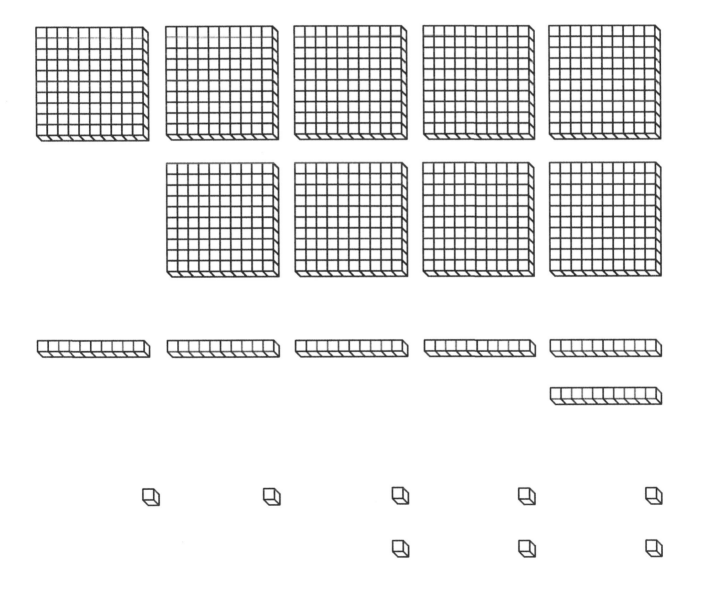

Congratulations - you are a driver!

Game materials needed for each company:

- ❖ Driver Sales Ledger (one for each player)
- ❖ One set of SALES cards per company
- ❖ End of Day Summary (one for each company for each day of play)
- ❖ One gameboard for the company and one game piece per player
- ❖ One calculator
- ❖ On Day Ten: one set of LIFE cards

Rules of Play:

1. Make sure the SALES cards are well shuffled at the beginning of each day.
2. Make a smaller deck with 18 SALES cards that will be used for today's play. Put the others cards aside.
3. Each warehouse carries 100,000 puzzle cubes. Puzzle cubes sell for $10 each.
4. Each driver starts each day with 10,000 puzzle cubes (10 unopened shipping boxes). This should be recorded on the front of each Driver Sales Ledger.
5. All players start the game by drawing a SALES card and reading it aloud. Players should not start doing their calculations until everyone has read their card, then all players work on their calculations at the same time.
6. Record all sales on the **Driver Sales Ledger** sheets.
7. Check your teammates' calculations to make sure that all company transactions have been recorded correctly and then double-check results with the company calculator. If you discover any errors, help each other find and fix them to ensure that your company books will have no mistakes.
8. After you draw the first SALES card and complete your calculations, look at the cubes remaining on your truck and round to the nearest 1,000. This will tell you where to put your piece on the gameboard. (Everyone starts at 10,000.)
   For example, if a player makes a sale of 836 cubes, they will have 9,164 cubes left on the truck. Rounding this result to the nearest 1,000 produces 9,000, so the player should move his or her piece on the game board to 9,000.

9. After placing their pieces, all drivers draw another SALES card (followed by calculations), until all 18 SALES cards have been calculated. This will conclude a round: one "day" of company driving.

10. After all 18 sales are completed, each driver adds up his or her total sales for the day and records it on the **End of Day Summary.** Double check your work by making sure that the sales and the cubes remaining on your truck add up to 10,000 and check the result with the company calculator.

11. Make sure the SALES cards are re-shuffled back into the full deck at the end of each day.

12. At the end of four days of play, calculate the total number of cubes your company has sold all together (checking the result once again with the calculator) and determine how much money you have in the company account (each puzzle cube sells for $10) and how many cubes you have remaining in the warehouse.

13. On Day Ten each company group will draw one card from the LIFE deck and calculate the final company total.

14. The biggest bank account wins!

Warehouse: _____ Driver: _____ Day: _____

Starting total of merchandise: _____ cubes

Unpacking/Repacking Area	Shipping Boxes	Pallets	Long Boxes	Loose Units	Use this space to add up the number of cubes you sold, repacking as needed to keep your truck organized.
Beginning Totals →	_____	_____	_____	_____	
Transaction:					
What's left on the truck					
Unpacking/Repacking Area	Shipping Boxes	Pallets	Long Boxes	Loose Units	
Beginning Totals →	_____	_____	_____	_____	
Transaction:					
What's left on the truck					
Unpacking/Repacking Area	Shipping Boxes	Pallets	Long Boxes	Loose Units	
Beginning Totals →	_____	_____	_____	_____	
Transaction:					
What's left on the truck					

Appendix G – Driver Sales Ledger (2 of 2)

Warehouse: _____ Driver: _____ Day: _____

Starting total of merchandise: _____ cubes

Unpacking/Repacking Area	Shipping Boxes	Pallets	Long Boxes	Loose Units	Use this space to add up the number of cubes you sold, repacking as needed to keep your truck organized.
Beginning Totals →	_____	_____	_____	_____	
Transaction:					
What's left on the truck					
Unpacking/Repacking Area	Shipping Boxes	Pallets	Long Boxes	Loose Units	
Beginning Totals →	_____	_____	_____	_____	
Transaction:					
What's left on the truck					
Unpacking/Repacking Area	Shipping Boxes	Pallets	Long Boxes	Loose Units	
Beginning Totals →	_____	_____	_____	_____	
Transaction:					
What's left on the truck					

SALES CARD Doug's Drug Store places an order for 77 cubes.	**SALES CARD** Zeli's Zoo is trying to raise money for an extra large elephant enclosure. They order 1,284 cubes.	**SALES CARD** Marcus Garvey High School wants to do a soccer fundraiser. They order 274 cubes.
SALES CARD Phineas's Pharmacy would like to order some cubes to see how they will sell. They order 193 cubes.	**SALES CARD** Gabe's Garage is giving away a cube with each oil change. They order 574 cubes.	**SALES CARD** Dr. Jackson's pediatric dentist's office is giving kids a cube if they are cavity free. They order 675 cubes.

SALES CARD Martin's Sneaker Emporium wants to place cubes around the store for customers and friends to play with while they wait. They order two dozen.	**SALES CARD** May's Market wants to have a special promotion for Arbor Day. She orders 849 tree-themed cubes.	**SALES CARD** A pop star loves puzzles and wants to sell cubes on her next tour. Her favorite number is 3. She orders 3,333 cubes.
SALES CARD Monica's Music Makers is giving away music-themed cubes to students who sign up for 6 months of music lessons. She orders 848 cubes.	**SALES CARD** Suli wants to design cubes that he can sell after his comedy show. He orders 783 cubes.	**SALES CARD** Elantra is trying to challenge the cube-solving world record. She needs three dozen practice cubes.

SALES CARD Soo is having a special party for her 29th birthday. She orders 29 cubes.	**SALES CARD** Ezekiel finds that working on a puzzle cube helps him get focused so he can settle into doing school work. He orders 14 so he can have one wherever he studies.	**SALES CARD** Penka's Pies is offering a cube along with every pie they sell on March 14th - "Pi Day". Penka orders 314 cubes.
SALES CARD Dave's Donuts wants a few cubes for their kids' play area. They order 27 cubes.	**SALES CARD** Rico Suarez, owner of a toy company, orders 59 cubes.	**SALES CARD** José's Jelly Bean Shoppe wants to create some custom jelly bean-themed cubes. They order 905 cubes.

SALES CARD Frederica and Lesa are throwing a puzzle-themed birthday party. They order 50 cubes for party favors.	**SALES CARD** Sharon's Surf Shop is holding a competition. Whoever can solve a cube puzzle the fastest wins a new surfboard and 10 free lessons. They order 284 cubes for all of the people who have signed up to compete.	**SALES CARD** Andrea's Apple Farm is having a party at the farm to celebrate their six-year anniversary. They order 2,660 apple-themed cubes.
SALES CARD Marco wants to give a cube to each of his nieces and nephews. He orders 28 cubes.	**SALES CARD** Diana's Dingo Rescue wants to educate people about the wild dingo in a fun way. They order 377 cubes with pictures and information about the wild dingo printed on them to distribute at schools.	**SALES CARD** Deshawn Is starting a private coaching business and wants something to remind people to work through their challenges. He orders 99 cubes.

SALES CARD The Museum of Contemporary Art is having a cube designing contest. Artists will complete their designs while people watch. The winners will have their cubes displayed in the museum's permanent collection. The museum orders 1,111 cubes.	**SALES CARD** Peter Piper's Pickled Peppers orders 442 pickled pepper-themed cubes as a promotion.	**SALES CARD** Mabel's Movie's orders 999 Black Panther-themed cubes for the movie's opening night.
SALES CARD Max's Mathletes at MLK High School are having a community fundraiser. They are selling cubes and hosting several classes on how to solve them. They order 1,970 cubes.	**SALES CARD** It's restaurant week. To encourage participation, the city is offering a nightly free meal to the person who can solve a puzzle cube the fastest. They order 375 cubes.	**SALES CARD** A sculpture artist is making a giant sculpture made of puzzle cubes. She orders 1,807 cubes.

SALES CARD	**SALES CARD**	**SALES CARD**
The mayor wants to boost his team's problem solving skills. He orders 1,295 cubes for everyone that works in City Hall.	Paul Bunyan's Summer Camp is creating an extreme obstacle course. In between each physical activity, campers will have to sit and solve one side of a cube before they can advance to the next obstacle. They order 329 cubes.	It's the United States' birthday! The fireworks commission orders 1776 cubes to give away on the 4th of July.
SALES CARD	**SALES CARD**	**SALES CARD**
Alex's Lemonade Stand orders 1,279 cubes to give away to people who donate to the Foundation for Childhood Cancer.	Finn's Fotos is having a photo shoot special. They order 789 cubes to give away to people who order their deluxe photo package.	Josh's Jamboree Music Festival is ordering Cubes to sell at their festival. They order 2,489 cubes.

SALES CARD Hal's Hamburger Hamlet wants to have a cube on each of the tables at their diner. They order 65 cubes.	**SALES CARD** Eva's Evergreen Tree Service asked for a special version of the cube to show their customers what different wood grains look like. They order 287 cubes.	**SALES CARD** Shannon's Sugar Shack asked for a special candy-themed cube to sell in her store. She orders 1,708 cubes.
SALES CARD This year's River and Blues Festival wants to order custom cubes with great blues musicians on each side. They are expecting a huge crowd. They order 1,073 cubes.	**SALES CARD** It's Chinese New Year! A local Chinese restaurant orders some cubes to pass out at the parade to advertise their restaurant. They order 699 cubes in different shades of red for good luck!	**SALES CARD** Simon's Soup and Sandwich Shop is ordering some cubes to advertise their new soup "Mushroom Madness." They order 74 cubes.

SALES CARD

A local artist orders 365 cubes to hand paint and raise awareness about climate change. She intends to give away one every day for the next year, starting on Earth Day.

SALES CARD

A local Taiko drumming group is performing at the Japanese Cherry Blossom Festival. They order 1,088 cubes to pass out at the festival.

SALES CARD

It's Diwali! The Patel family orders 82 cubes for their giant family celebration.

Warehouse Name: _____

Day of play: _____

Drivers: _____ _____

_____ _____

Day:_____	Total Cubes Sold	+	Cubes Left in truck	=	10,000
Truck 1		+		=	
Truck 2		+		=	
Truck 3		+		=	
Truck 4		+		=	
Truck 5		+		=	
TOTALS					

Total cubes sold: $_____

Total earnings for this day $_____

Cubes in the warehouse at the beginning of the day: _____

— cubes sold: _____

Cubes remaining in the warehouse: _____

New Warehouse Total _____

Drivers who checked this record: _____

Appendix J – Gameboard

Warehouse Name: _____

Truck 1	Truck 2	Truck 3	Truck 4	Truck 5
10,000	10,000	10,000	10,000	10,000
9,000	9,000	9,000	9,000	9,000
8,000	8,000	8,000	8,000	8,000
7,000	7,000	7,000	7,000	7,000
6,000	6,000	6,000	6,000	6,000
5,000	5,000	5,000	5,000	5,000
4,000	4,000	4,000	4,000	4,000
3,000	3,000	3,000	3,000	3,000
2,000	2,000	2,000	2,000	2,000
1,000	1,000	1,000	1,000	1,000
0	0	0	0	0

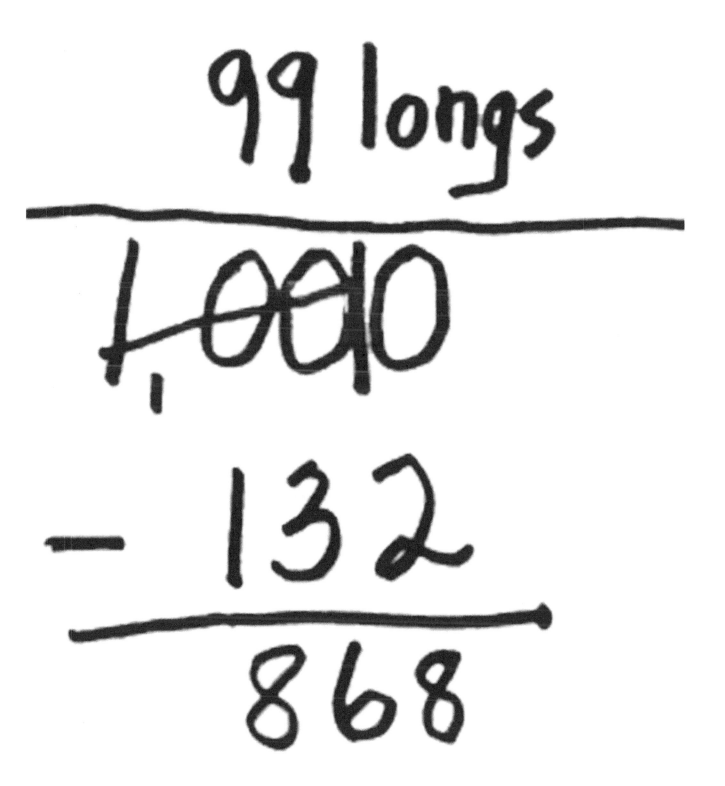

$$99 \text{ longs}$$

$$\frac{\cancel{1,000}}{-132}$$

$$868$$

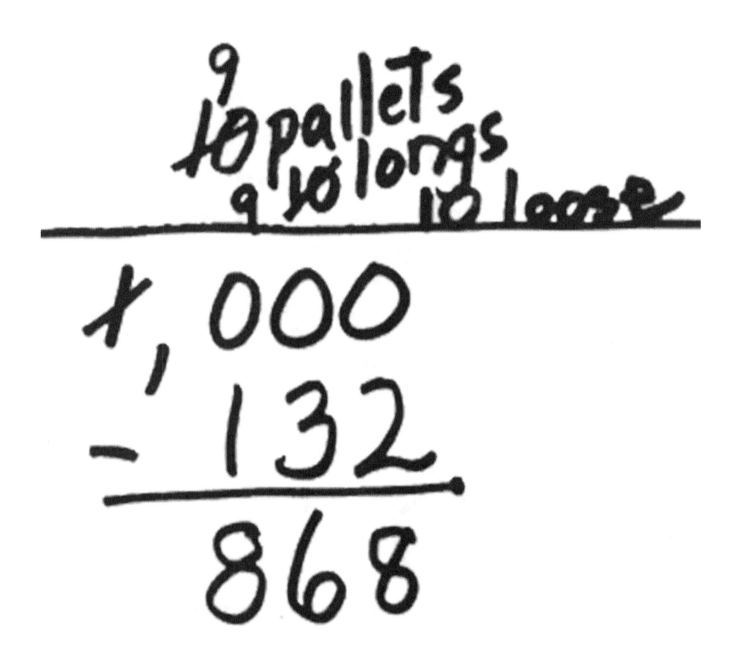

$$\begin{array}{r} \overset{9}{\cancel{10}} \text{ pallets} \\ 9 \overset{}{\cancel{10}} \text{ longs} \quad \overset{}{\cancel{10}} \text{ loose} \end{array}$$

$$\begin{array}{r} \cancel{1},000 \\ 132 \\ \hline 868 \end{array}$$

$$\begin{array}{r} = 132 \end{array}$$

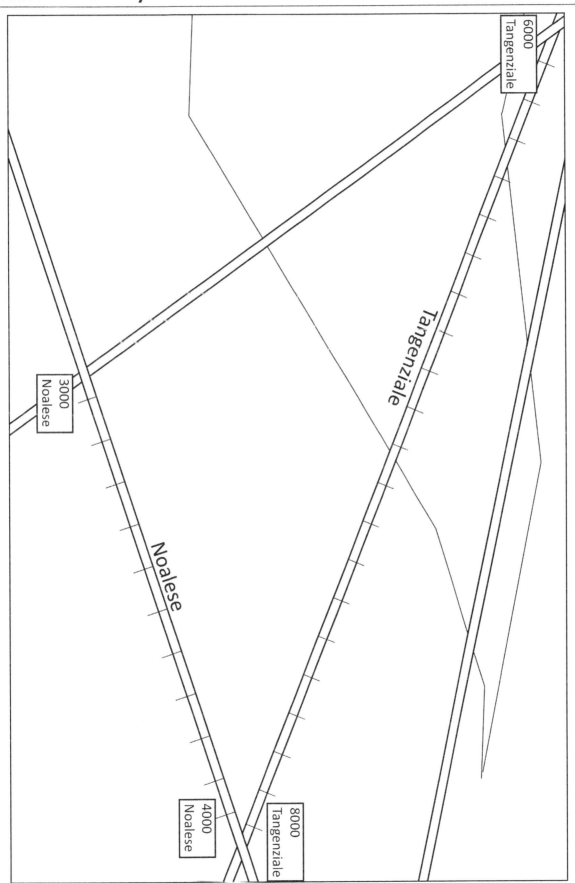

3435 Noalese	3022 Noalese	3964 Noalese
3179 Noalese	3218 Noalese	3748 Noalese

6131 Tangenziale	6545 Tangenziale	6936 Tangenziale
7264 Tangenziale	7246 Tangenziale	7739 Tangenziale

6858 Tangenziale	6431 Tangenziale	6222 Tangenziale
7045 Tangenziale	7099 Tangenziale	7582 Tangenziale

LIFE CARD You bring your very cute, fluffy dog to the warehouse as a therapy dog for your coworkers. While she is there she eats some packing material and damages several shipping boxes. Deduct $1,275.	**LIFE CARD** The air conditioning broke in the warehouse during the hottest time of the year. Repairs are needed, and it costs extra to rush the job. Deduct $1,435	**LIFE CARD** All the trucks need new tires. Deduct $1,000 for each truck.
LIFE CARD The company purchased new uniforms for the drivers. Deduct $200 for each driver.	**LIFE CARD** Oh no! A major storm hit the area and the company had some damage to the warehouse and needs to pay to have the grounds cleaned of fallen trees. Your insurance covers most of the damage but you need to pay the deductible. Deduct $15,000	**LIFE CARD** Woo hoo! New logos are being painted on all the trucks. Deduct $1,450 for the artist's design work and $200 for each company truck for the labor to paint the logos.

LIFE CARD The company donates $10,000 to a community charity. Word spreads that the company is generous and kind and sales double. Double the sales, then deduct $10,000.	**LIFE CARD** A water pipe in the warehouse bursts and damages several shipping boxes of cubes. Deduct $5,000.	**LIFE CARD** The company gives all drivers a bonus because of the hard work they did this year. It costs the company $1,000 per driver, but the drivers are happy, and they work to bring in more sales the following year. No need to deduct or add anything.
LIFE CARD The company donates 1,000 puzzle cubes to a robotics competition at the local highschool. One of the robots does the puzzle and breaks the world record! Word spreads and sales double. Double your sales.	**LIFE CARD** The company hires another driver. It costs the company $50,000 but the new driver makes $100,000 more in sales. Add $50,000.	**LIFE CARD** A driver has an accident. Luckily, he is fine, but the truck is not. The company needs to purchase a new truck. Deduct $50,000.

LIFE CARD	**LIFE CARD**	**LIFE CARD**
One of the employees had an idea for a new puzzle. The company built it and it is selling like hotcakes!	A nearby river flooded due to a very bad rainstorm and most of the company's remaining inventory was destroyed.	A bad blizzard hit the area and the 2 meters of snow dumped in the area causes everything to shut down for a week!
Add $130,000.	Deduct $1 for every cube left in the warehouse.	Deduct $12,000.
LIFE CARD	**LIFE CARD**	**LIFE CARD**
The company donates $1,000 worth of puzzle cubes to a community home for the elderly. One of the residents does the puzzle in under a minute and the local newspaper does a story on her. Sales go up by $5,000.	An investor who loves puzzles decides to invest in the company and gives the company $50,000 for some equity in the company.	It's the warehouse manager's 75th birthday. At the party you have an idea for a new puzzle using the number 75. The manager loves the idea and has 75 puzzle cubes made to commemorate his birthday. Each cube sells for $100 because they are collector's items.
Add $4,000.	Add $50,000.	Add $7,500

1,345 + 215	1,642 + 325	1,136 + 126
1,932 + 235	31,932 + 125	42,932 + 11,035

1,937 - 235	1,000 - 235	1,942 - 235
431,942 - 20,235	10,932 -10,322	1,932 - 275

Made in the USA
Las Vegas, NV
26 September 2024